BILL GARDNER: THE MAN, THE MYTH, THE LEGEND

Abe Atchia & Bill Gardner

© Copyright Abe Atchia & Bill Gardner 2020

All rights reserved.

Abe Atchia & Bill Gardner have asserted their right under the Copyright, Designs and Patents Act 1988 to be identified as the author of this book.
No part of this publication may be reproduced, distributed, or transmitted in any form or by any means, without the prior written permission of the author, except in the case of brief quotations embodied in critical reviews and certain other non-commercial uses permitted by copyright law. For permission requests, contact the author.

ISBN: 9798566542201

Typesetting by Socciones Editoria Digitale
www.socciones.co.uk

In Memory of:

Dennis Lepine

A life-long Hammer and Bill's mate for over 40 years

Service of Celebration for the Life
of
DUNCAN STUART MCGREGOR

6th December 1966 – 25th March 2019

Thursday 18th April 2019 at 12.45pm
Surrey & Sussex Crematorium

Service conducted by Jay Howells, Celebrant

Robert Daniel Brand

20th December 1953 - 28th September 2020

Friday 16th October 2020

St Margaret's Church at 1.30 p.m.
followed by the Burial at
Rippleside Cemetery at 2.15 p.m.

Contents

Acknowledgements i
Introduction 1
Mr West ham: Danny Fenn 4
Prologue: History Repeating 7
Foreword: Carlton Leach 13
PART ONE: Early Years 27
1. Birth After Death 29
2. Before the Storm 38
3. Cass Pennant 43
4. Get out Bill! Get out Before She Kills You! 53
5. Living with the Dead - An Introduction to the Gutter 58
6. Gypsy Gangs, Trafalgar Square and Pit Fighting 64
7. Boxing 71
8. Big Ted 74
9. Traced 83
10. Bunter Marks 85
PART TWO: Acceptance 105
11. West Ham Beginnings 106
12. Acceptance 109
13. Peterborough Tony 113

14. Me, the ICF, and the Truth 120

15. West Ham…United? 123

16. Frank McAvennie...127

17. Leaving Upton Park 136

18. Gary 'Boatsy' Clark (Nottingham Forest FC).......................138

19. To March or Not to March: The Real West Ham Fans Action Group 144

20. Emergence of the Newbies..150

21. Leipzig 152

22. Neil, Scobie, Lol 161

23. Man United with the Mile End Mob 179

24. Stuart Slater 183

25. Millwall: History and Hatred 194

26. Tough 202

27. Joey Williams (The Mile End Mob) 205

28. Collier Row...212

29. Palermo 215

30. Protection...217

31. Danny B 219

32. Enemies..228

33. New Definitions of a Hard Man...231

34. John Wraith (QPR)...234

35. A Trial, A Death & Abandonment.......................................244

36. Regret 255

Acknowledgements

Bill Gardner

I want to dedicate this book to my partner and soulmate, Sarah, who's had to put up with a lot from me for longer than I care to remember, and for giving me our two beautiful boys, James and Dan. Lads, you're old man thinks the world of you and loves you bundles. You've made me a proud man.

I'd also like to thank everyone who's contributed to this book: my old mates Ted, Bunter, Cass, Carlton, Joey, Lol, Schobie, Neil, Tony, Frank, Stuart, John Wraith, Boatsy and Danny.

As always, Steve Vaughn has been a stalwart and, without the combined efforts of him, Gary Northover and Abe wouldn't have got to have met up with my good friend Joey Williams, after 47 years.

Kevin at Sex, Drugs & Carlton Cole and Nigel Tufnell have been incredible in their effort and dedication, and as for Barry John Neville, who designed the fantastic cover, I'll always be eternally grateful.

I'd like to sincerely thank Abe – better known to me and a few others as Mozza - who's put in some proper graft on this project. During the course of writing this book he's had two ankle operations and worked on more stories than most journalists would ever dream of doing during these crazy times. Yet he refused to quit.

Lastly, but by no means least, I'd like to thank the West Ham family. You were there when I had nothing and, though you may not be seeing as much of me in the next few seasons, I've got enough treasured memories to last me a lifetime.

Look after yourselves,

Bill Gardner

Abe Atchia

Apart from echoing everything Bill's written, I'd like to dedicate my first book to my memories of the departed. My mum, Sarah, ex-partner and best friend, Marie Jeanette Sambucci, my cousin Richard, and Uncle Ismael.

I'd like to pay tribute to my dad, Ahmode, my two cousins Sarah and Aisha, Aunt Miriam and Cassim, as well as David Annis and Alison for putting up with my incessant phone calls, particularly on those days I wanted to launch the laptop out the window. I'd also like to thank Paul and Rozz who, coincidentally as my neighbours, would've been the first to spot the remnants of said laptop in their garden.

I'd like to thank Brian Massey for his long-time words of wisdom, Ian Wright (not that one) for his valuable feedback, and Steve Guy for his much-appreciated assistance in putting me in touch with some good people. I do also have to mention Justin at Socciones Editoria Digitale for service and help above and beyond the call of duty.

The boys in the Barking Vape and Juice shop wouldn't serve me again if I didn't give them a shout, as would my recreational manager, Rush.

Lastly, I'd like to thank Bill for giving me the opportunity to write his incredible life story. It's been a long old ride, but we got there in the end. I hope I did you justice mate.

Apologies to anyone I've inadvertently forgotten.

All the best,

Abe Atchia

COYI

I'd find it very hard to be hurt any more than I've already been hurt in my lifetime. I've lived a life where I've felt very much alone, misunderstood and, certainly in my early years, that no-one cared. The toughest battle I've had has been my life-long fight with my demons. To come out the other side of it I never resorted to drink and drugs. But I had to find a way out of the situation I was in. I found that at football.

Bill Gardner

2020

"*Some are born great, some achieve greatness, and some have greatness thrust upon them*"

Twelfth Night (or What You Will)
William Shakespeare (1601/02)

Introduction

This is not a book about football hooliganism. It is about the life story of its most important figure. That man is Bill Gardner. His race is Claret and Blue. His religion is West Ham United Football Club.

His story speaks of more than just a man who was once the saviour of many a West Ham fan. The autograph hunters and selfie-seekers, eager as they are to recapture both Bill and West Ham's glory days off the pitch, belie a tragic human story.

One of a vulnerable child who endured chronic childhood abuse, battles with mental health, unrelenting school bullying, bare-knuckle fights as a fifteen-year-old, teenage homelessness, and being taken into care.

However, it's also impossible to deny Bill's notoriety, infamy, and reputation as the 'top man' of Britain's terrace movement.

Much of British post-war social history is the story of baby boomers, mods and rockers, immigration, psychadelia, punk, new wave, Thatcherism, warehouse raves, street drugs, and the rise and demise of football violence.

A unique explosion of tribalism in the 1960s made its way from the terraces, to the streets, trains, ferries, and planes. By the mid-80s the phenomenon had a name – the English disease.

While Thatcher's storm troopers battled Yorkshire miners, someone, somewhere in Europe, was being kicked shitless because he wasn't an England fan.

Amid the crisis of the three-day week, hundreds of young men invaded towns, regions, and cities across England and the terrace homes of hated rivals.

As summers of love saw many tuning in and dropping out, the phenomenon was in its relative infancy, confining itself to the toughest of the tough. Small groups of men fought pitched battles before, during, and after matches.

No social media, policing, mobile phones, Sky TV – and definitely no 'firms'.

The reasons behind the terrace movement's rise and fall have been debated by many protagonists for many years. There has been much conjecture, hypothesising, and counter-argument.

This book will not join the debate seeking such explanations. It will, however, chart both the personal and terrace life of its most notorious and infamous figure.

In doing so, a deeper understanding of those three heady decades, whose influence continues to affect many today, may inadvertently reveal itself. If so, this is a welcome bonus.

But make no mistake.

With the unflinching respect and support of friend and former foe alike, this book is about being there. About living the life. About being the best.

Most importantly, it's about Bill Gardner: his stolen childhood and lost youth; his unwavering credo of loyalty, honour, and courage; and, invariably, his disgust at treachery and betrayal.

His unique status as one of the pioneers, originals, and archetypal 'last man standing'.

For many in the know, the name Bill Gardner has transcended football hooliganism and morphed into a mix of hard-man, terrace legend, cultural icon, and cult hero. He has been cited in books in pseudo-reverential terms and portrayed in motion pictures, including Carlton Leach's hit movie 'Rise of the Footsoldier'.

Yet Bill has rarely ventured down this road, turning down appearances on TV shows such as Britain's Hardest Men being just one example. His existence is a sparse and quiet one. It's how he likes it.

Getting him to open up about life as the terrace legend (a moniker he detests) of our time, therefore, has been no easy task. Harder still, and infinitely more painful, is charting the path which took him there.

Mr West Ham,

We've all hid behind him at 1 point or another
Especially when the proverbial was about to hit the fan
So i dedicate this simple verse to Bill Gardner
AKA Mr West Ham
Good afternoon gentleman was his greeting
In his own unique style
The man's as much a part of our history
As Greenwood Brooking and Lyall
He's probably clocked up more air miles than a pilot
In his quest to watch the hammers play
But i recently heard hes now had enough
And decided to call it a day
When a loyal part of our clubs fabric calls time
It shows our club is now rotten to the core
Cos he goes back to our golden era
Of Cassataris Peters Hurst and Moore
From Moscow to Palermo
The mans love for his club has shone through
No one could ever doubt his loyalty
Cos his DNA is claret and blue
An everlasting iconic image as Bill walked away from his church
When Bobby switched off the lights
Has now gone down in football folklore
As one of footballs saddest sights
If a picture could speak a thousand words
Then this 1 could write a book
As he solemnly walks away from his place of worship
Giving it 1 final loving look
The man deserves a testimonial

After a lifetime of unswerving loyalty
But to us fans he's the king
Our very own Boleyn royalty
Much like his namesake Bonzo
If you were in the trenches you'd want him by your side
Both never give nothing but 100 percent
And carry their colours with pride
So here's to Bill the claret hammer
The living legend the man
Our cement our history our heartbeat
But first and foremost a fan

Danny Fenn

Prologue:
History Repeating

It was a scene straight out of the sad, shitty '70s. Three bloodied Chelsea fans lay prone on the ground as hapless police officers rushed to the scene.

Above them, against a floodlit backdrop, stood the towering figure of their nemesis, West Ham United's top man, Bill Gardner.

They'd spotted him on the way back to the station after the game, decided to make their move and, as usual, had come off second best. Bill took no prisoners. They would have known that.

But the chance to bask in the tribal glory of being the first to take the scalp of all scalps had proved too much a carrot.

"A bottle came over and then the coins started. I knew straight from the off that I'd been spotted," Bill recalls.

"It was a cowardly thing to do. They also thought it was brave and manly to start spitting at me. If you want to fight a man, you offer him out. You introduce yourself, face to face, man to man. Throwing things from a mile away and spitting at people don't make you a man. It makes you a coward.

"There was a gap in the fence and, to be fair to them, the ones who wanted it were waiting for me. But you can't have Chelsea taking liberties at West Ham. You just can't have it. Not in my lifetime anyway. What disappointed me was there was only one other West Ham supporter who felt the same way.

"All the other West Ham fans were just walking past on their way to the station. Most of them were trying to pretend it weren't happening.

"One bloke stood alongside me, ready to take what was coming. Whoever he was, he has my utmost respect.

"Three of them came through the fence, and I just smashed the one who got closest to me first. He hit the deck pretty hard, and I remember thinking I must have caught him pretty flush because the knuckles on my right hand were killing me.

"His mates suddenly looked a little less interested, but that wasn't my problem. Two of them ended up getting the same treatment before the old bill arrived. I could've stuck the boot in, but that's not my style.

"If they'd wanted more, I'd have been happy to oblige, but I left that decision up to them. Once a man's had enough, he's had enough. End of. I've always believed that."

A scene out of the 'bad old days' indeed. But this particular run-in was as far removed from the '60s, '70s, or '80s as you could have envisaged.

This was 2017. Football had changed, leaving a groundswell of discontent among those who'd spent their lives following their team. It is arguable it had hit West Ham supporters among the hardest.

A fan base steeped in tradition which preceded the now infamous arbitrary decision to airbrush 112 years of history and move to "the next level" at the London Stadium.

And if you'd believed everything you'd read, heard or watched, Bill's ambush should have been a thing of the past, banished to a bygone age, making way for a game-day atmosphere where supporters now politely queued up, sat down, and inanely applauded their team.

No longer a game but a business, run more akin to market forces than the satiation of the heart.

Sanitised, soulless, sponsorship-led, and Sky funded, the English Premier League was now a product, a marketable commodity. Perish the thought that viewers in China, Africa, or the United States ever got wind of Premier League tear-ups.

This was the London Stadium, with its surrounding velodrome, funfair, Westfields shopping centre, coffee shops, and million-pound apartments.

The financial bastions of Canary Wharf and the Docklands stood proudly nearby, tangible symbols of east London's post-war rebirth and gentrification. They illuminated the canals meandering through the idyllic Olympic Park.

As Bill's encounter illustrated, some of the football-going fraternity were still hopelessly 'off message', and old rivalries die hard.

All a far cry from Green Street, the Boleyn Ground, the 'good old days'.

Gone was the splendour of the grandiose Boleyn pub, Green Street's illegal vendors, Ken's café, the ICF stalls, and the waft of burgers being dished out of dodgy looking vans.

Whether Chelsea would have attempted their little stunt had Bill not been spotted is conjecture. What is certain is that the name 'Bill Gardner' remains a focal point of conversation within certain circles across the country and beyond.

Turf Moor, October 2017.
Burnley 1-1 West Ham United

"We were on the coach waiting for the driver to get started on the journey back to London," Bill recalls.

"A Burnley fan got on, had a word with one of the coach organisers, looked up in my direction, and started heading towards me.

"A few of the lads were wondering what this fella was up to. This was a West Ham coach, after all. He had a youngster with him, and as he approached me, I could tell straight away he wasn't going to be a problem.

"I've always had good instincts, a sixth sense if you like. If it's going to go off, I pretty much know a few seconds before everyone else.

"Those few seconds have often been very precious, the difference between getting caught out and turned over or having the nouse to see what's about to happen and get the job done.

"At the height of the battle – and there have been a few – things tend to go into slow motion for me. I become incredibly calm, seeing things two or three steps ahead.

"So this Burnley supporter approaches me, with the younger bloke who turns out to be his grandson.

"'This is Bill Gardner,' he tells the nipper. 'And years before you were born, he saved my life.'

"In all honesty, I don't know the bloke and haven't got a clue what he's on about. But I did feel a bit guilty about him mugging himself off in front of his grandson like that.

"I waited till he started recounting his tale to a few of the lads on the coach before I leant down and had a quiet word in his grandson's ear. 'Take it from me,' I told him. 'Your grandad was never a runner. He stood firm and held his ground.'

"I don't know whether it's true or not. He might have bolted at the first sign of trouble. But I didn't want the kid thinking ill of the old boy, like he was some sort of coward. It wouldn't be right.

"It happens a lot. Over the years, I must have helped more people than Mother Theresa! 'Bill, you saved my life. Bill, I owe you big time. Bill, if it weren't for you, I'd have never made it out alive.'

"It's humbling, and I'm grateful. But I'd be lying if I said I didn't find it a bit embarrassing. Yeah, I've helped a few people out of some sticky situations, but that's just me. That's just who I am.

"I don't remember ninety-nine percent of what I get told. I'm just pleased that I was able to help someone.

"But deep down, it's embarrassing, and not something I look for. I'm no better or worse than the next man. I'm no different to any other bloke. It just boils down to my values. If I see someone in trouble, I'm not one to look the other way. And let's just say there have been a few times down the years with West Ham when I haven't."

Foreword

Carlton Leach

When Britain's football violence movement was at its peak in the '70s and '80s, Bill Gardner was its top man. It's as simple as that. Anyone who was there knows it's true.

Deep in their heart of hearts, top boys from firms across the country back then – many of whom I'm now friends with - know I'm right.

For the few travelling West Ham fans who'd go to away games, he was simply a legend. Someone they knew they could rely on to get them out of some grim situations, often against ridiculous odds.

That's why it was his name that the other firms always talked about, and why Bill was the one they wanted to hurt the most. But they never did. I never, ever saw Bill Gardner back down from anyone.

I'd started going to Upton Park around the same time as Cass (Pennant) in the early '70s. We must've been about 14 or 15 back then, just kids.

Standing on those terraces, you'd hear whispers of Bill's name without ever knowing who he was. He was like some mythical figure, often talked about but never seen.

I remember people would talk about what he'd done at the last away game in the same breath as the two big West Ham firms of the day – the Teddy/Bunter Firm (TBF) and the Mile End Mob.

We were a bit like kids talking in the playground and they were our heroes. But before long you graduate, and things start to get a bit more real.

The first lessons I learned were never run, stand your ground, and stick together. Kids like me turned out to be half-decent students and what we may not have achieved at school – when we bothered turning up – we more than made up for on matchdays.

I probably got noticed by the main faces when Manchester United came to Upton Park in 1975. It kicked-off pretty bad all over the ground that day.

I've never seen scenes like that at an English football ground since. I now know it was revenge for what happened in 1967, but that's another story.

Hundreds got nicked that day. I was in the West Stand next to the South Bank, which is where the away supporters would be. I remember seeing Bill steaming into the Man United on his own, and I did the same.

About ten coppers smashed me up quite badly, and I ended up getting carried out and nicked. My cherry was well and truly popped!

I first started seeing Bill at away games in 1976. We were all still buzzing off the '75 Cup Final and were now playing European football for the first time in more than a decade. I had to have some of that.

I remember Bill had long curly hair back then and looked a bit like David Essex. I used to do David Essex impressions at him and fuck about on the train, standing on the table and giving it large. Bill would just laugh and say something like, "Yeah, go on son".

I don't know why but he sort of took to me and said, "Come on, you're with us". I felt I'd become a sort of apprentice. It might sound silly now, but to a young kid that was a big deal. It meant you were alright, that you were accepted, that you were part of something.

From that point I was invited to travel to away games with Bill, Ted, and Bunter, travelling whatever way we could. Melvin from the Mile End Mob used to hire Transits and I'd be in the back, a 17-year-old kid thinking, "I've made it now, I'm with Bill Gardner."

Today's firms, such as they are, will never know how bad it was back then. The fighting on the terraces was naughty enough, but what went on outside the grounds, on the trains, walking back to the station... it was often do or die.

But Bill was always there, helping people, protecting West Ham fans, protecting his family as he saw it. That's why we held him in such high regard. He led by example.

Away from home us youngsters had a simple rule to stay safe and defend ourselves – follow Bill. You watched where he went, and you followed. No orders, no meet-ups, no words. You watched and acted.

Forget the police, especially the northern ones, who were virtually non-existent back then and hated Cockneys anyway. The best way to stay safe and give it back when it came on top was to follow Bill.

He was always so calm, assessing every situation, even with World War Three going off around him. At the same time, he was a ferocious fighter who'd back down from no-one.

My own life story is well documented and I'll say this straight from the off: there are very, *very* few people I've met who could've matched Bill Gardner for sheer strength, guts and courage.

For me it's simple - Bobby Moore was West Ham's leader on the pitch, Bill Gardner was West Ham's leader off it.

We can smile about those days now, but back then English football was a different animal.

Going to an away game you had to earn the right to get to the ground. Ninety-minutes later you had to earn the right to come back home.

You knew the home fans would be waiting for you outside. You knew it would go off. It was simply a case of how bad it would be.

You kept your fingers crossed you'd make it back, and that you were in one piece when you did.

Travelling with Bill you just felt safe, you felt you were in a safe environment and that you were part of an unbeatable force.

Eventually, the firm got bigger and grew around Bill. We were proud to say, "We're West Ham," and when we went to away games or London derbies with Bill, we felt we couldn't lose.

He had an aura about him and I thought, "This man's got so much fucking bottle. I want to be like him."

I don't think Bill ever chose to be that person; the leader figure we needed to bring us together. It was more the other way around - the West Ham fans chose him.

But I think he knew he had that presence and that he was the one we looked up to - Mr West Ham, as they say.

And could he have a row?! Fuck me was he game. I never saw Bill back down from anyone at football, ever. That includes the Mancs, Scousers, the other London firms, Middlesbrough, Geordies, the Midlands clubs, the lot.

Before you knew it, people were starting to talk about him outside of football: in pubs, clubs and at work. A reputation was being born, and I was glad to be there.

We weren't a massive firm in those days, but what we lacked in numbers we made up for in heart. We'd obviously get bigger turnouts in London derbies and the Midlands, but up north there were times when we'd only take a couple of hundred if that.

One year we got to Manchester United and went into their end, and we did the same at Sunderland as well, before getting sussed at the turnstiles.

Bill and me – Always loyal, Always there

Yeah, it was naughty, but end-taking was the be-all and end-all for firms across the country, and we were no different. And, wherever Bill went in, we'd go in, whether that was the home end or the away end.

As a result, it's fair to say I've been involved in some tasty battles down the years, with stunned home fans trying to get these 'Cockney bastards' out of their end.

An abiding memory I have of Bill was at Middlesbrough. They were a bit like us Boro, the West Ham of the north.

I was about 17 or 18 at the time, and there must have been about 50-60 of us trying to get in their North Bank. We mooched down to the away turnstiles, trying to keep a low profile.

As we were getting through the turnstiles it kicked-off between the Boro and West Ham firms in the street. The Old Bill had sussed us and it was truncheons at dawn!

While these days they'd have been nicked and probably spent the night in a cell, back then the police just frog-marched the West Ham into the away end.

The problem was Bill and me had already got through the turnstiles. I was looking around and couldn't see any faces I recognised, just Bill's. I was hearing all these people talking funny, not having a clue what they were saying.

I'll be the first to admit that it wasn't looking too clever for us. We had time to turn back but Bill wouldn't hear of it.

I told him what had happened outside and that we were on our own. "That's alright, we're still going in," came his reply. I thought, "Fuck me!" We made our way onto Boro's North Bank, Bill in his black bomber jacket, and we ended up in the middle of their end.

There were all these Boro fans milling around us as kick-off approached. Middlesbrough's main firm were coming in and I remember thinking to myself, "We're going to get fucking killed here."

But I was with Bill, and I wouldn't leave his side. He knew he could rely on me and I knew he'd look after me. He wasn't one for running, so I just waited for it to come on top.

All of a sudden Bill turns to me and says, "Fuck it." With that, he pulls his West Ham scarf out, holds it up above his ahead, and starts singing *Bubbles*! I thought we were both dead men anyway and joined in.

The pair of us broke into song at the top of our lungs. "I'm forever blowing Bubbles, pretty Bubbles in the air...!"

Straight away a big gap appeared all around us, and all I could see was thousands of Boro fans frothing at the mouth.

I'll be honest, deep down I thought, "This is it, we're fucked." It was only the adrenaline that kept me going.

But as ever, Bill was so calm. With that, it started to get a bit lively. Fists and boots were coming at us from all directions.

There was nowhere to escape even if we'd wanted to run. So all we could do was stand there and fight for our lives.

I got caught by a good few blows and gave a good few back. As for Bill, everything just seemed to bounce off him and was paid back with interest.

And then it was over. Just as quick as it had started the Old Bill turned up and hauled us down the front of the stand.

They took us over the wall and onto the pitch, before walking us around to the away end. When we got there, all the West Ham fans were cheering, clapping and singing our names.

I felt about 20 feet tall. The absolute bollocks! It's an indescribable feeling, one I'll never forget. "Thank fuck I was stuck with Bill," I said to myself, because I couldn't have fought with anyone better than him. In the West Ham end everyone was all over us. I felt like a fucking hero that day.

The Unwritten Rule

West Ham would always try to get into the Shed; Chelsea's home end. It was sort of an unwritten rule, and we loved it in there!

Around 1978 we were in a West London pub before our game against Chelsea. There must have been a couple of hundred of us in there, including Bill.

Me and some mates had got into a couple of rows along the way and got hold of a few Chelsea scarves off their lot which gave you bragging rights in those days. Taking the Shed that day wasn't going to be easy. To be fair to them, Chelsea had a tasty little firm of their own.

We got to the Shed turnstiles, and I was right behind Bill with Johnny Butler. We got through without a problem and made our way up that massive staircase towards the Shed End.

The butterflies were starting when we were met with a surprise.

There were a load of railings marking out the route to the top of the Shed. I'd never seen them before at the Bridge, and never since.

So instead of running straight up the stairs and steaming in like we normally did, we had to walk up, turn left, then right, and I remember thinking, "Where have all these fucking railings come from!?" As well as slowing us down, they were splitting our firm up.

We got to the top of the stairs but couldn't see any other West Ham. One of their spotters was there and he started piping up straight away.

"He's West Ham, that one's West Ham, there's another one."

As we got to the top he's shouted, "Gardner... Bill Gardner!" We followed Bill to the right, and they were waiting for him. They had all sorts: bricks, wood, metal poles, anything they could get their hands on, and they all just steamed into Bill. The whole Shed just went for him. We stood and had it with a few of them, but they really went for Bill that day, a load of them punching, kicking, battering him like their lives depended on it.

I jumped in and took a right-hander, Johnny Butler got whacked, and we were getting hit with bits of wood and all sorts.

But we had to get in there to save Bill. I remember seeing Jock steaming into them, trying to do just that.

It was like something out of a film. We couldn't and wouldn't let them take Bill. It was like, "You can't take the leader, we've got to protect our leader."

We weren't like them ones who'd just fuck off and leave when the shit hit the fan - no disrespect to anyone - and, the way I felt, there was no way I was going to leave Bill in there fighting Chelsea's firm on his own.

We jumped in front of him and, to be fair, we took more than we gave out. But it wasn't about taking the Shed anymore. It was about protecting Bill. We were prepared to take a kicking for him because we knew how many times he'd protected West Ham supporters when it had kicked off.

I think it says more about Bill than it did about Chelsea, what happened that day. The hatred they had for him was unbelievable.

I also think Bill remembered that day too. He's always been a man of principles, of values and helped so many fellow West Ham supporters, that I think it meant a lot that we were there for him.

The legacy that's surrounded Bill after all these years is incredible. I was recently sat on a plane quietly reading a book. The bloke next to me says, "Oh, I recognise you." To be honest,

I didn't really want to say too much, but he started telling me how his uncle was a staunch West Ham fan and a former ICF member.

So even though I didn't know the bloke from Adam, we started chatting about the old times, and it turned out he'd only ever been to West Ham twice, both times with his uncle.

Out of the blue, he said, "I remember my uncle mentioning a few names to me when I was a kid, but the only one who sticks out from the stories he used to tell me was a bloke called Gardner."

Whenever he mentioned Gardner's name he'd sort of whisper it; like it was a name you had to respect when saying it.

That sums up the way a lot of us, particularly the youngsters, used to look at Bill. Always the gentleman. He never took liberties and was always on hand to help any West Ham fan in the shit.

The Rise of the Footsoldier

I've often been asked about *that* scene in the first of the 'Rise of the Footsoldier' films, the one where some bloke is screaming at Bill through a terrace fence and ends up with a scolding cup of tea over his face. Well, it is a true story, apart from it being a cup of tea – it was Bovril!

It happened at Manchester City in the mid-seventies. There was around 150 West Ham stood next to the Kippax, which is where City's firm stood. As soon as they spotted Bill through the fence, they all came rushing over trying to get at him.

I thought they were going to rip the fucking fence down; not that it would have bothered us too much! So we improvised, and started using hot cups of Bovril and steaming hot pies as weapons. I remember Bill was at the front, and that's where that scene in the film comes from.

We did the same thing at Bristol City away when they got promoted to the old First Division. We walked into their end and there were hot pies and Bovril going everywhere. West Ham were split up and it was warfare everywhere you looked.

A Bristol City fan came up to me so I smashed a steaming hot pie into his face. I can still remember the bloke screaming his nut off with a sizzling meat pie stuck to his head.

As usual, Bill was at the front with everything revolving around him, like he was the centre of the Universe. Ted, Bunter, Scobie, and a few others were close to him. I was just on the outskirts of it, while the even younger ones were just beyond us.

Although it was carnage, there was a sort of order to it - Bill was in the eye of the storm and everything was happening around him.

But there was another reason I had to put that scene in the film. To be fair, it didn't need to go in. It wouldn't have changed much in the way of the storyline, but I wanted the world to see the man who made me who I am today. If people look up to me, I wanted them to see the man who I looked up to as a kid.

He was my hero. The man who, without a doubt, made the single biggest impression on me as a youngster. It was a statement, a sign of respect. I wanted the world to know who Bill Gardner was. That's how much he means to me.

Looking back, I suppose it couldn't have gone on forever, and when the arrests started in the mid-eighties, me and quite a few others started making alternative plans.

The London Stadium Move

The world and his wife know all about the response from West

Ham fans in the second season at the new stadium. It was a rough time with demos, protests and West Ham fan turning against West Ham fan.

There's more to it than that of course. But I do believe Bill was dragged into something under false pretences because of his name, and the respect West Ham fans have for him. He was dragged in and, in my opinion, used as a political pawn.

Those people couldn't lick his boots, let alone live in his fucking shadow. They know who they are, and they've got to live with what they did. Those in the know will understand what I'm saying. But for Bill to be used in that way was a fucking disgrace, and I know the whole thing upset him greatly.

If it came down to a choice between West Ham and Bill Gardner, I'd choose Bill every time. Don't get me wrong, I love the club. But Bill will always come first. And what happened over at West Ham after the move, well, there's only so much that can be said without raking it all up again.

I know first-hand what the West Ham family means to Bill. Back in the day, long before the ICF, you could be on a train with about 150-200 other West Ham, and you'd know virtually all of them by name.

You'd know their strengths, their weaknesses, the fighters, the jokers and the ones who might need helping out. It's strange how it worked, but it just clicked. We genuinely felt like a family unit, as well as a firm. For a few of them it was the closest thing to a family they'd had. My belief is that sense of family would never have come about without Bill's presence. For me, he was our father figure.

Those were the best days of my life. And if I could, I'd do it all again – the missed trains, the rucks, comradery, the coming back home a day late with two black eyes or worse —yeah, I'd do it all again in a heartbeat.

As for Bill, he's part of the history of the club in my eyes. Far more so than many of those overpaid players. I can't emphasise that strongly enough. He was his own man and didn't need a firm – ICF or otherwise – around him.

For me, just knowing Bill and standing alongside him is up there with winning any trophy… not that there's been too many for a while!

In my eyes he transcends the club and, that's how much of an influence he had on me.

It's very different these days, with CCTV, mobile phones, police escorts, and social media. But back then, going to watch West Ham away was effectively putting your life in someone else's hands.

Like countless others, I put mine in Bill's.

I'll be forever grateful to him for looking after it and helping me become the man I am today.

PART ONE

Early Years

1

Birth After Death

William Gardner's destiny was pre-ordained precisely four years, two hours and ten minutes before his birth.

On January 29th, 1950, Ann Gardner, the four-year-old big sister Bill would never know, died of leukemia. His parents, Charlotte and William Gardner, understandably shattered by the tragedy, would spend the following years consumed by grief, violence and mental breakdowns.

Bill's entry into the world on January 29th, 1954, at the same Essex home where his sister had died, was not the joyous occasion one would have imagined.

"They expected this lovely little, good-looking girl and instead of that they got big, ugly me," Bill recalls. "They never got over it. My dad had a breakdown and ended up having Electro-Convulsive Therapy. My mum lived in denial and rage."

"For a while, they thought I was Ann reincarnated. They'd dress me in pink and push me around in a pink pram. People I know have told me this. After a while, they stopped doing that, but growing up I always felt I was in the way."

Pain and trauma continued to hang heavy in the Gardner household, as inexplicable seeds of resentment, from those he looked to for protection, began to bear fruit.

"It wasn't a normal childhood by any stretch, but it took me years to see that. They were always at it; the rows went on forever. My dad never ever laid his hands on my mum, never; it was always her hitting him. I used to see the tears roll down his face. Even as a five-year-old I knew it wasn't right. I'd just sit under the table crying when they started up."

By the age of five, Bill had become the brunt of his parents' discontent and frustrations and was subjected to verbal, psychological, physical and sexual abuse.

"They used to hit me with a broom handle and when that broke, they'd cut the broom and put tape around the handle, so it was like a Japanese riot police baton. They used to permanently whack me with that.

"They also had this plastic thing that used to go over the old butler sinks. It was like a decorative thing, but it was thick plastic and that used to hurt more than any wood. It used to sting, and they used to belt with that as well.

"I can never remember, even from a young age, either of them giving me a kiss. I can never remember my dad putting his arm around me. I can only remember him watching me play football once. I was 26 years old, and it was my last game. I'm so proud he was there watching that last game, and I scored.

"My mum used to put a wedge between us, so we could never really become friends. Everything was too aloof. I believe that those years, my early years, especially when I was on my own, had a massive impact on my future life. I used to have to think on my feet all the time to escape a beating, or worse. Mentally, it was exhausting.

"I used to talk to myself a lot. I never answered myself in a different voice or anything like that. But I believe I was bipolar from a very young age. I was never diagnosed with it, because I never went to the doctors.

"But there were always two sides to my character. There was 'good Bill' and 'bad Bill' - the angry one.

"In my younger days, and especially at football, 'bad Bill' was much more prominent. It was a constant battle keeping him at bay. I put that down to loneliness of those early years, of spending so much of my time alone and afraid.

"At that age you don't know any better. It's not something you rationalise or think about. It's normal. Your mum and dad bring you up a certain way. As a child, you don't have a clue whether it's right or wrong, healthy or harmful.

"You're totally dependent on your parents. If they said this is how it goes, you aren't going to question it, are you? You don't know any different.

"It's easier nowadays. You've got Social Services; you talk to them, they take you away, they give you foster parents, you get looked after to a certain degree. In my day there wasn't any of that. You were a good boy or a naughty boy, and that's where it ended. This is why it's taken so many years for a lot of these people who were child abusers to come to light, because in those days there was nothing there. Absolutely nothing. They'd have never believed a child, anyway.

"There was no-one I could turn to. No-one. That made me stronger, but I've never felt, in my whole life, that there was anyone I could turn to.

"In the end, it takes away your willingness to trust people. From the age of 14, when I left home, I've always relied on myself. If I got in a hole, I tried to dig myself out of it. It's not easy. Sometimes you're strong and sometimes you're weak.

"I came to learn my homelife was wrong through epic battles with my parents and within myself. Before leaving home in my early teens, I could go from anger to sadness to guilt on an hourly basis. But, like I say, I thought that was normal.

"I began to realise things weren't normal when I started school. Yeah, I was big, fat, and bullied for a good few years, but that's not what struck me.

"I had no confidence and was shy as fuck. I couldn't speak to the other kids and I found it difficult making friends. I looked at other kids and would think, "How come they're so happy when I'm not?"

"How come they can speak with such confidence, shout and play while I'm just sat here not feeling able to join in?"

"I was self-analysing myself at a very young age, something no child should find him or herself doing.

"On one of the rare occasions I spoke to someone at school, I asked a boy what sort of cot he slept in. He gave me a funny look and started laughing.

"I sleep in my bed silly," he replied. I was shocked.

"At the age of eight, I still slept and spent most of my time in a pink cot. It was in the corner of my mum's bedroom. When I wasn't having my tea, that's where you'd find me; playing imaginary games and, as time moved on, teaching myself to read and listening to the radio.

"I loved horror films from an early age and remember peering over the edge of the cot late at night, on my own, watching Boris Karloff in *The Mummy*. It scared me shitless, but I was fascinated by that fear. The victim in the film was like me, scared. I just wanted to help her.

"I wondered how something on a small black and white screen could have that effect on me. I was savvy enough to know he wouldn't get me but was still scared rigid nonetheless.

"That fear would return to haunt me with a vengeance in the East End cemetery I would later call home as a teenager."

Ann Gardner

"I've always felt a connection with Ann. I never met her. I never spoke to her. We never played together. But she's always been a part of me, a guardian angel watching over me. All I knew was that I was born within ten minutes to the day, four years after her death. The chances of that have got to be a million to one. My mum and dad were always tuned into how long she'd been gone, and I was always being compared to her, even though she was dead. I suppose it was natural I'd end up growing up with a sense of there being someone else living with us.

"When they were bashing me with the broom handle, or a lump of plastic pipe, or trying to get me with a breadknife, or abusing me, I had no-one. So sometimes, when I was on my own in my cot, I confided in her. That made me feel better when I was a nipper. As I got older the West Ham family took Ann's place. But I've always considered her a part of me.

"I think my mum and dad would've accepted me if Ann had lived. They would still have had her, so I'd have been left alone and safer. For everything that happened, I don't blame my mum and dad. It's the hardest thing in the world to lose a child. Horrendous.

"When you lose a child, like they lost my sister, it takes a bit of getting out of your system. She wasn't a day old or a week old, she was four years old. It's a massive thing for any parent to lose their only daughter as a child. I can't imagine the pain they must have been in.

"But you've got to be intelligent enough to say, in my instance, this baby who's arrived now is not a little girl, he's not a carbon copy of the girl who died. But it affected them. My dad couldn't get Ann out of his head.

"As for Mum, I could've asked her, "How long's Anne been dead?" She'd tell you by the years, the months, the weeks and the hours. She really could. She dwelt in the past, which to her was more important than anyone's future, including mine.

"They'd clothe me and feed me, but there wasn't the affection that a father or a mother should give their child. I never had that.

"My mum was OK to me in front of other people, but behind closed doors was a different matter. There was a lot of resentment that I lived, and Ann died. It was said to me a couple of times when I was about eight or nine. "I wish you'd died and Anne was here." That was my mum. My dad never said it, even if he thought it.

"To everyone looking in, my mother was a good caring mum and at times she could be. But then there were the other times when she wasn't. I didn't know what was happening when she sexually abused me when I was 7 years old. What kid that age does? I didn't know the difference. She'd be smiling when she done it, so I just thought that was normal for me and every other kid. I was wrong about that. As I got older I ended up becoming a bit of a loner, which was never something I intended. I was happier in my own company, and didn't trust a soul.

"My parents are both dead now and I still go to their graves every three weeks or so. I change the flowers, clean their graves, tell them I love them and tell them I'm sorry. There's always been a part of me that wonders if I could have been a better son; that maybe I could've done things differently. I don't believe I was a bad child. I never brought trouble home, the police never knocked on our door, but obviously, I wasn't quite what they wanted.

"When you grow up being told you're nothing, you're worthless, your dead sister was a much nicer person than you...I suppose it does things to the way you see yourself and the way you feel about yourself that might be wrong. But you feel them anyway. You feel them even though you don't understand why you think about yourself like that.

"I've always taken responsibility for everything, good or bad, whether it was my fault or not. I don't know why I have, that's just the way I am. The same applied to my childhood with my parents. As much as it was their responsibility to look after me when I was a kid, it's now my responsibility to look after them.

"But there's plenty like me. There's plenty who've had it worse. Maybe I'm the only one in who's prepared to admit it, though that's taken a long time. I loved them. I love them now. I haven't abandoned them. Their graves are the cleanest in the graveyard. I always put colourful flowers on because my mum was always over the top with colour. I go up there, and every time I stand there, I apologise.

"I have no ill-feeling towards them. They had their lives to lead, and I now have mine. They must have done what they thought was right at the time, although some of the things were very wrong. But I can't blame them for the way they lived their lives, what with them losing my sister. I just wish I'd been intelligent enough, and grown up enough, as a teenager to see what they were going through and to ease that burden on them.

"I always wanted to go football with my dad when he went, and always wanted to be around my mum. Every now and then we used to have a laugh. She had a good sense of humour. But my dad was very withdrawn and that was down to what happened to my sister. I enjoyed being with him. But I always had the feeling he was on another planet. I was their son, they would've looked after me, they would've cared for me, but I always think that hurt never left them. So, I can't condemn them for suffering that pain, because I've never suffered it myself, and I wouldn't know how I'd react.

"A lot of the time I thought for them to be so unhappy with me, I must be doing something wrong. I didn't want my mum and dad to have an unhappy life. They'd lived through the war; my mum had worked in the war effort.

"There are certain feelings that won't leave me alone - it was my fault; I could've fixed it, but I didn't. I can't get rid of that for some reason. I've always taken the can for everything. I will take the can for anyone. I've never grassed on anyone; I never would grass on anyone. But I've always felt that because of the way that my life's been, it's been my responsibility to try and cover for other people. To try and help as many people as I can in the way I lead my life. I think Cass summed it up in the book when he said I was the fan who became the man, who went back to being the fan again. Along those lines, I agree with him 100 percent.

"The life I led in the middle − on the terraces - was maybe not the life that I wanted, or the life I would have chosen. But it was the path that I walked down, and I take full responsibility for that. At football, I got the respect that I never got at home, or anywhere else.

"I liked that feeling, though as the following pages will describe I sometimes liked it a little too much.

2

Before the Storm

To say my mum had a temper is an understatement. I suppose, in all likelihood, she passed it on to me. My mum would fight anyone. She had no fear whatsoever. The flip side was my dad's calmness, which I also inherited. Nothing much fazes me, up to a certain point.

When I do lose my rag, however, as I've done many times over the years, things sort of slow down around me. Sounds become distorted and my eyes sting. I've been told by those I've fought with – and a few I've fought against – that my eyes turn a demonic red, and that, for some reason, I've usually got a grin on my face.

Uncle Ted

One particular morning I remember lying there in my cot in my mum's bedroom. It stood next to my mum's bed and I felt it being shaken. I peered over the top and this bloke was looking at me while he was on top of my mum. I don't know exactly how old I was. Being in the cot didn't mean anything in my family - I might have been fuckin' 21!

The bloke and my mum knew I was there. They knew I could see them. There he was, giving me mum one and I thought,

"Who's this strange man?" When he saw me watching them, he put his finger across his lips as if to say, "Shhh."

"Hello there mate, why don't you just go to sleep?" he'd say, and I always did.

He was introduced to me in time as my Uncle Ted, and my mum had a thirty-year affair with him. She had nothing to do with my dad. They always slept in separate rooms.

My dad knew all about Uncle Ted, but there was nothing he could do about it. That didn't help him. It only occurred to me recently, but I never did know my old man before they pumped all that electricity into his head. He might have been a completely different bloke. As it was, he was living on a different planet. Against all the odds, I grew up to become really good friends with Uncle Ted. He was a decent bloke, working as a lorry driver for the water company. To be fair though, I did make his life hell when he always tried to fuck me off out of the way so the pair of them could go at it.

So, I used to play the game. When he was round our house I'd say, "There's some good stuff on at the pictures this week."

Quick as a flash he'd say, "Oh you fancy the pictures, do you? Want to go to the cinema?"

"Yeah, but I ain't got no money," I'd reply.

"That's alright, I'll treat you. How much do you need?"

"I wouldn't mind an ice-cream as well, if that's alright."

His wallet would come straight back out. "There you go, have that for an ice-cream."

Before long, I'd up the ante.

"It's gonna be really cold when I come out. Any chance of fish and chips?"

Out came the faithful wallet and off I went for a nice night out with a nice little wedge in my back pocket. I didn't feel guilty about it. I just thought, "Well fuck me, he wants me out of the way to give her one, so why not?"

As usual, I'd go on my own, but it was a good little scam. I'd come back home, have something to eat, go to bed and get under the covers with my crystal radio and a book, trying to match the words up.

My dad would be at work at the Ford factory in Dagenham at the time. He worked nights and would get back home around 8:45 in the morning, right about the time I was going off to school. We didn't really see each other much.

Those feelings of not being wanted, of being in the way, got worse the older I got. I started going through a cycle of sadness, anger and guilt. It was mentally knackering.

The bullying at school was also becoming increasingly worse. I had virtually no sense of self-worth. Self-respect, confidence and self-esteem were completely alien to me.

I was recommended to be seen by a hypnotherapist when I was 11 years old – only the second child of my age to do so in the country. I felt the benefits almost immediately after a couple of sessions.

I don't know how it worked. It wasn't like I left his office clucking away like a chicken or anything. But my mood, and in particular my confidence, took a distinct turn for the better. I felt like a different person altogether.

Up until then, I'd found it very difficult to make proper friends. The only proper mate I'd had was a kid my age called Bobby Ackhurst, who lived six doors down from me.

It's impossible not to remember Bobby because even though we were good friends, playing football and whatever, we would also have some proper tear-ups.

I don't just mean little kids and handbags. We'd fall out over something petty and then start bashing each other up with bricks, pieces of wood, spikes, metal; whatever we could get our hands on.

Those fights could easily go on for an hour or so and became a regular thing with us. We'd play footy, fall out over a disputed goal, and then smash seven bells out of each other. After we'd had it out, we were best of friends again.

But we did used to go at it! I remember on one occasion the pair of us lying face-up, side-by-side, on the cool spring grass in Hornchurch Park.

Christ we were a sight! There was claret all over our faces, bruises, grazes and lumps and bumps on top of lumps and bumps. Scattered around us lay pieces of wood, stones, a metal bar and some bricks. We were breathing pretty hard. We were bloody knackered.

We picked ourselves up, dusted ourselves down, and went up to Hornchurch Hospital. The face on the nurse who came out to see us was priceless.

"Good god!" she shrieked. "You two *do* know the war's been over for a while now?" We just sat there grinning at each other the way naughty kids and best mates do.

Before long we were on our way home, strapped up and plastered. I remember having my arm over his shoulder while he had his over mine.

We both knew it was bound to happen again. We also knew if anyone bothered either one of us, the other would be right there by his side sticking up for him.

I often wonder what became of Bobby. If he's still alive and reading this, I wish him all the very best.

By the time I was turning 14, the rows and the beatings I was taking at home were getting worse. Dad turned a blind eye to it, although in fairness there wasn't much he'd have been able to do. Not with my mum at any rate.

In this day and age, I suppose the social would've been down asking why I'd been missing so much school. If they had done, I reckon I would've been taken into care there and then.

However, these were different times. Everyone fended for themselves. Kids like me from working class east London or Essex areas were no different.

It was a ticking time bomb leading up to an inevitable conclusion. I just didn't know what that conclusion would be.

How could I? I was a kid living in a very adult world, with very adult activities going on right in front of me. The rows, the beatings, the cheating, the constant tension, it all built up within me. Mentally I was in a shit place and drained.

Speaking now as a father of two grown boys, I can see it was a very dysfunctional existence. But back then it was normality. A way of life I tried to ignore and suppress.

That said, I knew it couldn't go on like that forever. Thoughts of leaving home plagued me, but also tied me up in knots as I didn't think I'd have the bottle to make it out there on my own.

As my 14th birthday approached, I could sense a big, final storm brewing.

I didn't have to wait long before it arrived.

3

Cass Pennant

There's a saying that goes 'You can't take the boy out of the man'. But Bill was never a boy. He was always a man: *the* man, amongst boys.

For loyalty, courage and honour he bled claret and blue, and I should know. I've known the man from the early '70s. As a teenage North Bank boot-boy, events once got the better of me. "What's going on?" I asked.

Everyone had piled round to Castle Street when there was supposed to be an in-house straightener (a fight, to the uninitiated) between West Ham and Mile End, who were West Ham's top firm.

Thankfully, it never materialised. But a name was whispered all the way back to us schoolboy teens. "Gardner. Bill Gardner." In the coming seasons of working my way up the ranks, I learnt more about who Bill was. I learnt from him, and I respected him.

I was also proud to have got to know him and his family outside and away from the football.

Many think of or see him as Mr West Ham. I understand that totally, for he was not just respected, he was loved by those that went both home and away.

For all that, Bill was a very private, reserved man. Someone who never saw himself in the same way we did. I remember once having a private conversation with him that became a bit of a heated debate. I said, "Bill, you was the top man and the true leader of the ICF." I added his firm was the TBF (the Teddy Bunter Firm). I said it to him only because many of us had said it and thought the same thing.

"Cass," he replied, "you're wrong on both counts." He went on to crush the debate by challenging me with a few words of his own.

"When did you ever see me in the pubs with you lot before a game at home? When did I ever go on the hunt up Euston with you lot after any home games?"

He was right. When you look back, he always came alone. It was us – the ICF – who wrapped ourselves around him as a firm.

You had to be there to know what it was *really* like back then. If you can remember those away games up north, fixtures so grim and dodgy, it felt like it was only the firm that was travelling up to those games back in the day.

You would watch the home end stand emptying out before the final whistle. When the 90 minutes were up you had to head back to the station, back to London. But that home end that had emptied out before the whistle went, well, they would be waiting outside our end.

So, you'd watch people make their moves, working out who to follow, and who to hang out with, and then you'd hear those whispers.

"What's Bill doing? Where's Bill?" And the classic, "Wait for Bill!" Bill would still be rooted on his feet in the ground somewhere. Your eyes would pan the crowd, and then you'd spot him. Blonde hair, scarf around his neck, black leather jacket, burly and well-built.

Then, without any commotion, he'd just walk off, and like the pied piper the ranks would just fall in behind. It wasn't like there was a weakness on the part of the fans. After all, it was often only the east End's finest that went West Ham away in those days. But when you talk about someone having a presence, well, Bill had it in buckets. Simple!

Me and Bill having it large

The best example I can give of this was when he walked in the Chelsea Shed end one season when end-taking was still the be-all and end-all. For a good few of us, it was the reason we went. I watched from being within feet of him how he stirred up a hornet's nest while fronting Chelsea's firm up by announcing himself in style. "Good afternoon gentlemen, the name's Bill Gardner."

He said that to Chelsea, in their end, with them all around him. Some of us had got in too early, ahead of our main firm who had been sussed out at the turnstiles, so just a few of us were in.

I was close enough to hear the murmurings from Chelsea's boys who were searching us out. I could hear them saying, "Find Gardner. Find Gardner and you find West Ham." But many hadn't realised he was stood amongst them, in their end. It was a crazy thing to say at the time because say what you like about Chelsea, they had a naughty firm. Why else would we be there?

I thought we were well and truly outed if we hadn't been sussed already, and in no position to defend the forthcoming onslaught. But Bill is some strategist and, believe me, Chelsea just froze and pushed the pause button. Then it was panic, chaos on their side.

We then rallied around Bill and went into them and what followed takes longer to write than describe. We got smashed right out of the Shed as Chelsea went mental out of embarrassment and Bill's audacity, the front he'd given them.

The police opened up the turnstiles to let us out and that's when you could see we just didn't have any numbers. Our full firm was still lurking outside in the courtyard, smarting from being thwarted at the turnstiles.

I'd taken a few digs, a few of us had, while others inside who'd tried to join us in support ended up getting kicked out with us. Our pride was definitely wounded but we were all chuckling. Bill's actions would forever add to his legacy. For me, it was just enough to say I was there to witness that immortal line: "Good afternoon gentlemen, the name's Bill Gardner."

It might have looked pure show but I was close enough to learn something about his psychology. You knew he meant it, and seeing the first reaction of the startled Chelsea boys told you *they* knew he meant it.

OK, so Chelsea gave us a slap when we were outnumbered. But when the boot was on the other foot, well, you can throw all that 1990s fair play Hollywood crap out the window. Back in the day, if I'm being brutally honest from my experience, it could shift from naughty to serious to dangerous in the blink of an eye.

But it wasn't just West Ham. Back then, if you got on the wrong side of firms like Millwall you could end up on a drip-feed, or worse. So, imagine the situation going back to 1974, when less than 100 West Ham had gone in the Cold Blow Lane home end at Millwall, taking up a position behind the goal.

We were surrounded on three sides by home fans, desperate not to let Millwall get the upper hand by getting round the back of us. We held them for the whole first-half, before one mighty push from them finally broke our lines.

In truth, there was no more than forty of us, if that, because a good few West Ham numbers had slipped away unnoticed while those who remained battled for our lives; fighting to stay on our feet.

Our numbers had become small enough for the police – who in the absence of stewards were mainly matchday volunteers back then – to get involved, and they finally seized their moment to get us out of the Millwall end.

Then I saw Bill. He was still pushing back, trying to get back in their end as the Old Bill pushed us back, truncheoning us down a big flight of stairs at the back of the Cold Blow Lane stand.

The police tried to nick me at the top of the stairs but let me go as Millwall tried to go through the Old Bill to get at me. I quickly walked out onto the street. I had to catch the lads up.

I was surprised they were still milling around before realising why. A firm of ours, who had only one thought, had surrounded a couple of Millwall faces you'd certainly think twice about messing with.

The look on the Millwall pair's faces was priceless. "Oh fuck, you lot ain't Millwall are ya?" Cue West Ham laughter in reply. Wicked, evil laughter. They'd come unstuck. We knew, and they knew, what was coming next. It wasn't going to be pretty.

That is until Bill stepped in, fronting us. "Anyone who lays a finger on them has to deal with me," he said, without needing to raise his voice.

I remember thinking that was incredible. Like everyone else, I was thinking that no way would that happen if things were the other way round; if it was two West Ham surrounded by Millwall. This was just moments after everyone was still smarting from the battle we'd been having with them in their end.

There were a good few West Ham up for revenge, and these Millwall lads were certainly game enough and not looking for any favours.

Mercy didn't happen in them days. But it did that night, so they walked.

It was an act that stayed with me as I was to exercise the same restraint on more than one occasion myself over the years. It was a lesson learned, and it marked us apart from other firms.

It must have been hard on Bill. He hated Millwall with all his breath, but he was to do the same again when a Millwall lad mistakenly got in the same train carriage as us in the '80s. That was just the way he was. He didn't see the honour in it.

I've known Bill long enough to know he had a somewhat difficult relationship with his father, who had his own thoughts on Bill going to football.

Never more so than one cold January morning of 1987, when Bill's name was all over the papers after being arrested during the dawn raids of *Operation Full Time*. So here we were. The West Ham eleven. It was a big story because it was the same series of police operations that had seen the Chelsea lads go down for 10 years in 1986.

What was especially worrying was the fact that these show trials bore political overtones, and were designed to send out a message to the world - Britain was sorting out its football hooligan problem.

It also followed the aftermath of the Heysel tragedy, when all English clubs were banned from playing in Europe. In truth, they were five years too late for the likes of me and Bill.

We'd considered ourselves long retired, and Bill was not up to much as he had a broken leg, and was isolated from the rest of us as we were all refused bail. When on remand, word was getting back to us that Bill was struggling within himself and needing proper treatment on his leg. Unfortunately, he was in the same boat as us: locked up in a cell 23 hours a day.

The next time we were to see him was when we were brought together for the start of the £2.5m trial; 15 months after those dawn raids. It was to last three months at Snaresbrook Crown Court.

The outcome was sensational. The trial collapsed when the prosecution stated they no longer had confidence in the integrity of the police evidence against us. We were free to go and my immediate emotions were of both joy and anger.

We had proved to the entire world that we were stitched up by the police. If anyone hadn't believed us in the beginning, with all the headlines being written about us, then they had better believe it now.

Except it wasn't the same for Bill. His dad died during the trial, and he would never know his son was proclaimed totally innocent of all charges relating to violence at football matches.

As co-defendants, we considered ourselves winners by nature, even though the odds were stacked against us, and our lawyers proved in court there was political interest in our trial.

Even police officers suspended from duty were allowed to give evidence against us, which was unprecedented because they themselves were defendants in another trial, charged with the assault of Gary Stretch in November 1987. An attack so brutal he received £10,000 compensation in 1994.

We all really felt for Bill in our 'punch the air' moment of triumph on hearing the prosecution's words. He'd had a lot to deal with emotionally with his father's poor health and eventual death.

It affected his mother too, as well as his own health because of the lack of exercise due to his broken leg.

He'd ballooned in weight but, despite his own grief, was always looking to keep everyone's hopes and spirits up, particularly the young lads on trial with us, as we shared the cell and dock together during those testing months.

He knew how we all looked up to him, so he was never going to reveal the true extent of suffering the trial was having on him and his family.

The judge said we could go. So we went out the front way of that grand courthouse, and headed for the Britannia pub in Plaistow to celebrate - followed by the news crews.

Bill, however, quietly slipped away and went home. A lot of people have never understood the man and a lot more besides. He was his own man. We had wrapped ourselves around Bill and not the other way around. A real fan, a real legend, a real friend.

But if you didn't know him, were ever in trouble, and you were wearing claret and blue, he'd be your best friend too.

The West Ham fan loyalty to Bill is 100 per-cent genuine. When the rumour mill started a few years back about Bill being ill, there was a lot of sincere concern.

None more so than from one of the main TBF lads who rang me asking if I'd ring Bill's house to see if it was true that Bill was dead. The fact I'd spoken to Bill just a few days earlier was irrelevant - I was not going to make such a crass call. Think about it. "Hey Sarah, is your husband…well how can I put this? Dead?" Thankfully Bill pulled through fine. We were now entering the new millennium, and Bill had a lot going on health-wise.

Personally, I don't think he ever fully recovered from the many health issues he went through with the ICF show trial. You know when Bill has a problem because he won't ever miss a game, home or away.

So, one home game I suggested us all putting on an evening in Bill's honour, to let him know how highly we all thought of him.

Everyone thought it was a great idea and it was all done in the spirit of cheering Bill up, and signalling our appreciation of him. Bill can be quite reclusive by nature, so there was no guarantee he would turn up to the bar we'd hired in the West End, with band and DJ's booked.

But he did. As did some 200-plus fans in a night many of us still recall because, aside from it being a top night among our finest, Bill kicked off the evening with an opening address after the call of, "Speech! Speech!" rang out from a packed bar.

Bill got to his feet.

"I know you all thought I was dead," he said. "Well I'm not! And for those interested, I've got news for you. I'm going to be around for a good few more years yet!"

That's Bill all over: Straight, sweet and to the point.

I remember asking him once, while we were doing a chapter for the book *Terrace Legends*, who he respected from our rivals. Surely there must have been someone I thought.

He looked me in the eye before replying; as if he was giving it serious thought.

"Cass," he said. "They was two bob, the lot of 'em."

4

Get out Bill!
Get out Before She Kills You!

January 1968,
Hornchurch, Essex

I'll never be able to pinpoint how or why this particular row started, or why it became the breaking point. I've often tried, but always failed to understand what happened that night.

It could have been Mum had lost some money that day. She was a big gambler, and she'd back anything that moved. She won £8,000 on the pools in 1962. It was a lot of money back then, but all went back to the bookies within a year.

It could've been something else entirely. A row with my old man or Uncle Ted, or something I'd done or said to upset her earlier that day.

It could've been something to do with the hysterectomy she'd had - when she threatened nurses before walking home in a bloodied top. She'd later told us she'd seen a dead body on the ward.

It could've been one, none, all, or some of these things. At the end of the day, I don't suppose it really matters anymore.

What *did* matter that night was the large bread knife tearing a hole through the wooden bedroom door. I watched as it pierced the doorframe, cowering on the floor with my dad.

I remember the blade reflecting against the ceiling before disappearing and reappearing, over and over again. We'd had to lock the door. It would've been madness not to.

Her screams were unforgettable. I can still hear them now. She was ranting at the top of her voice, to the point it was unintelligible. I remember thinking the police would turn up. That a neighbour, maybe Billy's parents, would have called them. But it wasn't like that back then.

I can't pretend I wasn't scared, but I couldn't cry. It wasn't for the want of trying either. I just couldn't. My dad, on the other hand, was in pieces, sobbing away next to me on the floor.

"You've got to get out, Bill," he told me. "You've got to get out before she kills you." It sort of made up my mind for me, which brought a bit of unexpected relief in the chaos.

"If I could just get through tonight," I thought to myself. "If this would stop, or she'd calm down, or just get knackered and go to bed, I'd have a chance."

One night a few weeks later the house fell silent at around 9:30 pm. I think my mum had fallen asleep in an armchair in the living room. I decided to take that chance. I tiptoed around the bedroom, gathering up a few things and stuffing them into a few shopping bags.

I was on autopilot. Not really thinking too much about what I was doing, where I was going, what the effects would be. I wanted out, and not just out of the house, but also out of the manor.

I just wanted to disappear, to go to a place where no-one knew me, and I didn't know them. Deep down I felt anonymous, and I was alright with that. It gave me a strange sort of comfort.

I thought about waiting for my dad to come home to say goodbye, but decided against it. It weren't worth the risk if she woke up and caught me with my carrier bags packed. I left home early that morning, while it was still dark and before the District line trains started up. In my bags were a few items of clothing; a radio, some books, a torch, and my Swiss army knife. I didn't know then how much I'd come to depend on that knife, but I'm bloody glad I took it with me. I made the walk to Hornchurch underground station and waited for the first train. It was bitterly cold, and I put my hands in my pockets and gripped that knife so hard it hurt.

My shopping bags lay at my feet and my breath seemed to pour out of me for miles, sort of like a steam train. I didn't feel free, relieved, excited or any of that bollocks.

It wasn't an adventure or a game. I'd outgrown those kinds of feelings long before then. There was no sense of a new start. There were no 'final words' ringing in my ears, no sense of destiny, no smiles and no tears. There were very few thoughts to be fair.

I was simply at a station, waiting for a train to take me somewhere different from the one I'd just left. End of.

I didn't have a clue where I was going to end up, but that weren't important. If I had to describe it in those sorts of terms, I was just doing the rational and safest thing I could.

Looking back, that might not make a lot of sense to some people. I think it's fair to say I was blocking a lot of stuff out. The enormity of what I was doing as a 14-year-old kid didn't hit me until much, much later.

In later years I've tried reaching out to that kid. I've tried to understand what he was feeling back then. But it's impossible.

As I'll go on to explain, I believe the years of abuse I suffered had a definite impact on my mental health. There were certainly two sides to my personality. I'd probably spent too much time on my own and become too used to being comfortable in that zone. As a layman, and knowing what I know now, I certainly think I had something of a split personality.

That's something I've managed to keep from anyone but my nearest and dearest for many, many years. There was the 'calm Bill', the nice one, the intelligent one, and the bloke who'd give you his last quid if you needed it.

But then there was the 'other Bill'. The "warrior Bill". The one who'd take no shit from anyone, no matter who they were, where they came from, or how many of them there were. Many of the people who know me best will often describe me as a loner or, if they're being kind, 'my own man'. They're right to an extent.

When I think back to the days of the ICF, the TBF, the Mile End Mob, and whatever, I've always said I didn't need to be in a gang.

With the wisdom of hindsight, I think it's more the case that I didn't *want* to be in a gang, and that if I put my trust in other people, I was always liable to get hurt.

West Ham fans became my family, and I'd defend them to the hilt. But it was on my terms, no-one else's. That way I ran far less risk of being hurt or being rejected. I didn't think a lot of myself. A lot of people may be thinking what's he going on about?

What I'd say to them is have a good look in the mirror and ask themselves if they like the person they see. For many years I wasn't able to do that and say 'yes'.

As for that kid, waiting for the train that freezing morning at Hornchurch Station, there was no joy, sadness nor fear. There were no feelings at all. They would find an outlet but would only come to the fore, quite literally, a little way down the line.

5

Living with the Dead
- An Introduction to the Gutter

January 1968,
Aldgate, East London

At the age of 14, Bill Gardner was implored, and acquiesced, to leave the family home for his own safety. It would be the last time he would run away from trouble, the futility of standing his ground on this occasion self-evident. Uncertainty clouded a bleak future. Bereft of any clear direction, he effectively moved under the radar; not in school, of no fixed abode, confined to a hand-to-mouth existence. He was, for all intents and purposes, 'persona non grata'.

A desperate war with increasingly frenetic inner demons ensued, as did mentally exhausting attempts to salvage belonging, self-worth and understanding from the wreckage of the world around him.

The year I spent living on the streets as a 14-year-old kid was easily the worst time of my life. But it was still better than being at home. I had no preparation for homelessness, and it was my introduction to the gutter.

I spent a few nights sleeping in shop doorways and one night in a hostel, but soon knocked that on the head. I didn't want to be picked up by the police and sent back home.

The hostels were a nightmare. They were full of pissheads who'd nick anything off you. I woke up one night and found some geezer going through my bag. I gave him a clump and think I knocked him out because he was so pissed. I like to think he slept well that night!

I couldn't have any more of that. When I stumbled across the cemetery at St. Botolph's Churchyard in Aldgate, I thought I'd give it a go. I'd been on my feet and in doorways for three days straight. I reckoned this would do me for a couple of days if I kept my head down. I ended up living in that cemetery for a year. I'll never know why I felt comfortable there, but again, it was better than being at home. It felt peaceful being surrounded by a sea of graves.

The first few weeks were spent bawling my eyes out. There were more questions than answers. What was going to happen to me? What were Mum and Dad thinking? Were the police looking for me? Would I survive it?

I didn't have any answers to those sorts of questions. What 14-year-old kid would?

West Ham kept me going. I'd only been going on my own from the age of 11 and was there for the battle against Manchester United at Upton Park in 1967. I'd met a few good people who I still know today, but I wasn't going to tell them I was living rough. I didn't see the point. This was my life, my shit, my issue to deal with. It was no-one else's business.

Thoughts of being back amongst them kept me going a lot of the time. Many a freezing night I'd fall asleep, shrouded in cardboard and plastic sheets, thinking of our next game.

I'd sleep in half-hour slots because of the strange noises that would wake me up: a car horn going off and police sirens going past. I'd hear the rustling of the trees and think, "Who's this coming?"

But never once did I bow down and ponce money off of people. Not once. I've got a bit more dignity than that. It's very hard for kids because they think London's streets are paved with gold. They're not. They're paved with nonces, sex cases, and all kinds of people. In the year I was on the streets I was propositioned 11 times by well-dressed men in pinstriped suits. They'd have loved to take me home, give me a nice home-cooked meal and let me have a nice bath. But I knew the score, and although a couple of times I was so cold I was severely tested, I never ever succumbed. I never lowered myself like that.

It's the cold that kills you. Imagine sitting fully clothed in a tub of ice-cold water, then trying to sleep, wringing wet, outdoors on a winter's night.

In the end, the tears and the fear disappeared with me and I just wanted to go from day to day. After a little while living rough I got used to it. I got used to the icy wind, the bitter cold and the piss-heads.

I slept close to some railings I could get through. I covered them with a bush so that nobody could get in there and it was a bit safer.

It's hard thinking about that time, let alone talk about it. But it made me the man I became.

A Stranger in the Dark

I woke up in the cemetery one night and a geezer was sitting on the bench opposite me. He had a huge beard. I thought, "Fuck me, who's this?" Before I had a chance to open my mouth he said, "How are you? How long you been here?" I told him everything, I properly opened up. I was bawling my eyes out.

Then he says something really corny. "You'll never be beaten, but you will die a terrible death." I was taken aback. I thought, "Oh fuck me, here we go, another nutter." I got up to give him a slap.

When I looked up, he'd gone. I thought, "What's happening here?"

I went to the hole in the railings. It was still covered.

Who was it? I'll never know. Another rough sleeper? Very possibly. To this day I don't know how he got in there, or how he got out. It was strange, but it drove me on because I've remembered his words all my life. I've never felt I could be beaten in a fight. Never mind the odds. Never mind your reputation. And bar one exception, the bloke was right.

My One and Only Defeat

Romford, 1971

When I first left school, I went out drinking in Romford with the painters I was working with. I've never been a big drinker, but the blokes I was with were going at it hard. So, I had ten pints of Guinness and was off my nut. What I didn't know was they'd put half a bottle of methylated spirits in the Guinness. I got outrageous with another group of lads slightly older than me in Romford High Street.

I'll be honestly truthful with you, it ain't me, but I pulled a knife out on them. It was wrong, but it was the booze. A week or two later I'm standing on the edge of the road opposite where I lived, and these cars pulled up. These geezers got out, about five of them, I think. I didn't recognise them.

One of them come up and said, "You don't remember me, do you?" I went, "No", and whack, he's clumped me and we started fighting. He said, "I was the one you pulled a knife on in the High Street." I remembered who he was.

I decided not to fight my corner. What I'd done was wrong. Going round with a knife isn't me. So, I let him give me a couple of slaps and it was all over. I wasn't on the floor, I was still upright. They went away, and I went home. But I deserved what I got because I was wrong. I shouldn't have done that. I've never done it since. They came from the Racecourse Estate in Hornchurch. I don't know this bloke, but if he's still about I want to apologise. That wasn't the way I operated. I was out of my head and ill in bed for three days after that. They shouldn't have done that to a young kid, making him drink all that shit, but I was impressionable and wanted to fit in. That was the first and last time I backed down from anyone. I didn't care who you were or how many of you there were.

It was around then the tough, angry side of my personality really came into his own. It toughened me up and made me more resilient. He began to dominate the side of me that was feeling sorry for himself, who wanted to cry, who didn't see a future. He made me see this isn't right, but you've got to box on. It's difficult to understand unless you've been there yourself and spent that much time on your own. My life-long mental health issues were made at home, nurtured at school, and nailed shut on those streets.

When I heard about a Gipsy crew who might have some labouring work, I wasn't a sniveling kid anymore. He was gone. Warrior Bill was in charge, and it's a good job he was. I was about to enter one of the most brutal stages of my life at the age of 14.

6

Gypsy Gangs, Trafalgar Square and Pit Fighting

Although only 14, I looked like a 20-year-old and had the strength of a man. I used that strength, I used that experience and nobody saw me ever have it on my toes at football. I stood; no matter what the odds or how many there was.

Ask Millwall about Whitechapel Station in 1972. West Ham had just played Chelsea. There were about 30 Millwall on the platform picking off West Ham fans as they got off the train. Ask them how many West Ham got off the train and went into them and they'll tell you. One. Me. Two of them I knocked out completely cold, they were laying on the floor comatose. But there was too many of them, 30 people is far too many, it can't be done. They were all kicking each other and I was jumping between the seats covering myself up. I could feel a few blows then it all went quiet. I thought, "Thank fuck they've gone." I went to stand up and got a boot straight in the face. But I only had a little cut. It was unbelievable I got away so lightly because I could've been stabbed easily. I would never have known who'd done it and they would have all covered up.

It if happened now I'd be dead. But not back then.

Manchester United fans – the one's who were there back then – will tell you the same. I don't back off, I don't step down. I won't see West Ham supporters taking shit off of other fans. I suppose you get a bit of a reputation after a while. You meet real friends, and you meet people who might just like you for what you've done. In those days I just wanted people to like me, so whether they were real friends or not I don't know, but I took them at face value, as I have always done with people. Sometimes that can come back to bite you on the arse, other times you've made a friend for life.

Earning a Crust

An Irish Gypsy outfit was looking for labourers. I had nothing, so needed to start earning quickly. The job was perfect, although backbreaking. No pension, no P45's, no questions asked and no guarantees. On a busy morning there'd be as many as 100-200 blokes queuing outside Finchley Road Station; the pick-up point, and it frequently kicked-off. You can't blame a bloke trying to feed his family, but there were a few liberty takers I gave a clump because they made out they'd been picked instead of me. I didn't feel good about that, but it was survival of the fittest.

I'd be up at 5:00 each morning, usually frozen and soaked to the skin, to get one of the first trains out from Aldgate. They used to pick us up at 7:00, so I just used to go there and wait. Some of the crews used to have different workers every day, but the Gypsies I worked with had me most days because I was a hard worker. They used to tell me, "We need you tomorrow or we don't need you tomorrow," so you knew you had a bit of work or not the next day. I did everything while working for them. Loading gear, pushing wheelbarrows full of tarmac, pushing a big mechanical roller which compacted the tarmac. After a while, I was driving lorries for them. I must have done 65,000 miles without a licence! When I was a bit older and took my test I'd had eight lessons and the examiner asked me afterwards, "How many lessons have you had?"

"Eight," I replied.

"Amazing!" he said. I thought, "Yeah, but I can't tell you they were in a 20-tonne truck bombing around Trafalgar Square!" I was alright with the Gypsies. I worked hard and they could give me a job and be confident I'd get on with it. I had a bit of savvy, and they saw that.

If they sent me to the van for a sledgehammer, I wouldn't come back with a spade. It wasn't like what you hear about now, with slavery and people being kept in a caravan and made to work for nothing. They paid me every week, and I had no arguments with that.

It wasn't a regular job, but there weren't much work about for a 14-year-old boy. If I worked for 5 days with them, I used to get a tenner. If I didn't, it'd be less. But it was enough to get something to eat, to get washed in the local swimming baths, and enough to go to West Ham.

I'd later find out my dad was Gypsy. When his family came to the funeral there were loads of people with horse-shoe rings on and the usual trinkets. My parents had kept it from me because he'd mixed outside his race and married a 'gorger', or foreigner. His parents disowned him for it.

Pit Fighting

Nowadays, people go down the gym and have all these steroids to build muscle. I had nothing. I didn't go to the gym. My work was all the lifting I needed to become strong.

The Gypsies noticed me. They could see I was a big lump, a hard worker, and no-one's mug.

"Blimey, you're strong," one of them said to me one day.

"Well, that's just the way I am," I replied.

"Why don't you fight? Don't you want to earn big money?"

"How big's big?" I asked.

"Two thousand pounds."

I was getting £10 a week, so £2,000 was an absolute fortune for a 15-year-old kid.

"What have I got to do?" I asked.

"You have to have a fight."

"Who with?"

"Could be anyone."

At first, I thought, "Fuck me, I might be well outta my depth here." But I had great belief in myself and I knew I could hold my hands up with anyone at that time. I didn't care who they were or where they came from. I would only fight for money or if somebody had hurt anyone of mine; my friends or family. And that's still the way I am today. I consider West Ham fans as my family. They stood by me when I had nothing.

The Gypsies were offering a hell of a lot of dough so I thought, "Fuck it, I'll have a go."

"Alright," I said, "where's the ring?"

"No ring, in the ground, in the pit," he said banging his pitchfork into the earth.

It's not the way a 15-year-old kid should live. It's brutal, and it's not Marquis of Queensbury rules when you're down in that hole. The bloke opposite you is frothing at the mouth. He wants to do you because upstairs he's got a load of wedge to pick up when he beats this young boy across the other side of a fucking 12ft by 12ft pit dug into the middle of a field.

They'd go to a farmer and say, "We want to use your field. We'll put it back in the same condition it's in afterwards." They only used it for a couple of hours a night because there were no police in there, it was private property.

So they get somebody to come in with a JCB, he digs a pit - 12 ft by 12 ft deep - and they give you a ladder. You climb down into this trench, down to your trousers or your jeans. Your shirt's off, and once both men are down there they pull the ladder up, and you fight. Simple as that. The first one unconscious, or who gives in, loses the fight. The other one goes up the ladder and picks up the winnings. Two of my four fights were in and around St. Albans in Hertfordshire. I think the same farmer let his field out twice, and what the different Gypsy groups used to do was stand around the edge of the pit. They used to have money on who was going to win. I was the underdog cos I was the young kid. They put me in with one bloke who, fuck me, he had no nose. It was flat. But you ain't gotta worry about the one with the flat nose, you gotta worry about the one whose give it to him. I used to look across the pit at them and I could tell, I just had this instinct I was gonna win. I could smell it. You can see it in a man's eyes. When people look at me they don't see that look. While I was down there the punters would be watching from up top and betting loads of dough. I was getting two grand for this. At the same time a professional boxer was earning 300 pounds for a pro fight.

I had four pit fights and won them all. There were no rounds. You fought until one man was beaten. They used to do them in the summer so that the cars and the vans could park on the field without getting bogged in. You don't do it in the mud because it fucks the field up, so they'd do them in the good weather and you'd get in and have your row.

I won't lie, I was fucking nervous before my first fight. You feel those nerves till you're actually in the hole and you see who you're up against. You look across. These were men I was fighting. Every one of the people I fought was at least 10 years older than me. There were no youngsters. And yeah I was 15 but I was strong, very strong. I was 6 ft 3 tall, weighed 13 stone and was all muscle. And you go at it. You go at it hammer and tongs. Looking back, I was fortunate.

They're all the same to start with, both of you steam into each other. In my first one I was a bit apprehensive and I waited for him to start. He come into me, I side-stepped him, I caught him with one that shook him, and when I knew I could hurt him I thought, "Fuck this, I'm really gonna hurt him." So I kept on banging away at him and the bloke, to be fair, was quite strong and a big lad. But he didn't really catch me. I dodged out of the way quite a lot and eventually I caught him with three big punches that put him down. He put his hands up. He'd had enough. That was it. Because I was big and strong I had a knockout punch in both hands. I've always relied on both hands equally. But I've got no knuckles anymore. They've vanished.

People will say it's horrific, and they're right. It's no way for a kid to grow up. It was all about the dough. I made so much money off it. I went to work the next day, and then back to the cemetery that night. I gave myself a few little treats for earning that money. I bought myself some clothes, new trainers. I gambled a bit, went to the dogs, went horse-racing, and in a strange way look back on that time with fondness, even though that's not how it felt at the time.

7

Boxing

Boxing teaches you respect and honour; the two most important characteristics I look for in people. After having the pit fights, I gave it some serious thought. I worked for a wine merchants in London, and one of the blokes I worked with was the former professional heavyweight, Billy Wynter. He was ranked 26th out of 30 and came from Antigua. After work, we used to go to a place called Oxford House in Bethnal Green where we had our own gym. I must've been around 17, and he used to bring people in to spar with me. No-one came twice. They only ever turned up once. Some of my mates at the time thought it'd be a good night out and a laugh. It didn't work out that way!

Billy started getting pro-fighters for me to spar with. One was Ron Lyle, an American pro who I sparred with many, many times. He was an American fighter from Ohio and rated one of the top five heavyweights in the world at one stage. He went on to fight Muhammad Ali for the World title in 1975, but I think he was outclassed on the night. I believe his fight with George Foreman in 1976 was one of the best fights of all time. Ron had just come out of prison when Billy first brought him down the club and I first sparred with him. After that, whenever he used to fight over here or in Europe, I used to be his sparring partner. I must have done about a thousand rounds with Ron. I did reasonably well against him. I sparred with a few others who were pros, but never really made names for themselves. It was a great time. I really enjoyed it. I liked it because you only get out of boxing what you put in. You have to work hard. I used to run about five miles, four mornings a week, each time with some bricks on me back in a pack.

I used to be in the gym four nights, and I used to have Sunday off. That lasted a couple of years. I was with my first wife then, Leslie. She used to come and watch, and we'd go out afterwards. She was always on at me to have a drink, but I couldn't drink. I was in training. I'd always ask for a 'bitter lemon,' but she wouldn't have it. She'd carry on and on, and I succumbed. One drink led to two, two led to three, and suddenly I wasn't getting up in the mornings and I wouldn't do the running I needed to do. So, it sort of petered out.

That I regret. It wasn't her fault; it was my weakness. I have a lot of regrets. I wish I'd have stuck in there. I don't think I'd ever have been a champion, but you never know. I would certainly have had a go. Fighting in the street is a lot different to fighting in the ring. When I was sparring with Billy, I hit him so hard once it would've knocked most blokes out cold. With Billy, I ended up busting my hand on his head! They had to cut the glove off me, and I ended up going to the Royal London Hospital for ultrasounds twice a week to break the tissue down. They said when I got older I'd get bad arthritis in my hands, and that's what happened. I've managed to lose all my knuckles along the way!

Most boxers have broken hands. Most have had, or will have, broken hands. It's part and parcel of the sport. It's like a rugby player with a thick ear. Boxers have busted hands and fingers. I've busted every one of them down the years: busted them, dislocated them, and generally fucked them up one way or another.

Boxing and Today's Kids

Today's youth should be doing things like boxing, of course they should. The Government stopped funding youth clubs, they stopped funding community centres where kids could go, and coaches to coach them at different sports. So, the kids congregate. They end up on street corners and get up to no good because they're bored. A lot of older people moan at kids. 'Bloody kids' and all that, but kids need something to do and something to aim for. Myself and Cass offered to go round the schools in Newham trying to get kids on the straight and narrow. The police never even had the decency to contact us and say, "Thanks, but no thanks."

8

Big Ted

One of my funniest memories with Bill was a midweek game at Derby away in the '70s. We were part of a group of about 20 West Ham who went up there by coach.

Everyone on the coach were good people, and no one wanted to get nicked because it was work the next morning. We'd come out of the ground after the game and as we're walking along to go to the coach, a big group of Derby supporters were waiting for us.

But there was another gang with them, some black fellas. They were stood there in the street staring at us. Then out of nowhere, they started running up and down doing kung-fu kicks, roundhouses, all that martial arts stuff that was pretty big back then.

Me and Bill were up the front. The others had piled in behind. I think we were all thinking the same thing while watching these 50 or so geezers. I thought, "All very pretty lads, but what you gonna do?" This Derby, West Indian, kung-fu mob obviously thought they were going to have a go at us, while we just stood there staring them out.

It was surreal and it was funny. They just wouldn't stop doing those fresh-air kung-fu chops and kicks. I suppose they thought we'd be intimidated and run.

We weren't laughing at them but it was funny all the same and very strange.

With that, someone said, "Let's go," and we ran at them. They bolted! Just ran away! I don't think I laid a punch on anyone to be fair.

Bill 'The Magnet' Gardner

I've always called Bill the magnet for Spurs supporters. He's not got much time for them, and they hate him, they really do. I don't know how that started. We'd been going there having fights with them for years, and going back to the old days when we would go in their end. But for all the effort Spurs have put in down the years, they've never done West Ham. I know. Bill and me have been in the middle of it every single time.

The night we beat them 4-0 at their place when Psycho got four goals, sticks out. We just flooded the place. There were so many of us. That was probably the best night I've had down there. It was so packed and we were in the Park Lane End.

To cut a long story short, we've come out and it's kicking off everywhere. Some of their well-known people who hated Bill were on the other side of the road. There was about 10 or 15 of us, and one of them threw a bottle over towards us. He then comes over to have a go. I'll be honest, I was really up for it that night.

Anyway, this bloke, I can't think of his name but he's was of one of their leaders, came towards me with his arm in a sling. I gave him the 'come on then' and with that, he pulled a knife out of the sling. As soon as he done that the Old Bill turned up, let him go, and nicked me!

Fortunately, I had a load of witnesses there and went to Magistrates Court, where you never get a not guilty. But I managed to do exactly that. It makes you laugh. I was going to have a fight with the bloke and then he pulls out a blade.

I don't even know if there was anything wrong with his arm!

Obviously, the Old Bill didn't see the knife, but I did, and they just jumped on me. I spent most of the night in Tottenham police station, and they let me out when they knew I couldn't get home. I gave Scobie a call and he picked me up and took me home. That's the way it was. We looked after each other.

The problem with me and Bill is that because we're big, we're going to be the first ones to get pulled, spotted, or attacked. It's amazing he's gone all this time without being done in court like I have. Maybe he's just cleverer than me!

It's fair to say Bill's built up a lot of enemies from Tottenham, among both old and young.

I honestly don't know the reason why they despise him so much, but I assume a lot of it dates back more than 40 years. Over the last 10 years, whenever we've gone there, I've said to him - because he would go there on his own he's that hard-headed! - I won't let him down if I go with him. He's got his own people but I like to be safer than sorry. So I've always said, "I'll come with you and I'll make sure there's a few with us who won't run."

It's a fact of life that Bill needs more help now. In the past, no way. But it's just a matter of pride. So I always make sure I'm with him for Tottenham away with who won't have it away on their toes.

Since we got promoted in 2011 and we've been going over to their place, we've always met at Barking Station, then took the little train line to South Tottenham. It's a long old walk from there to the ground up Tottenham High Road. We've done the Liverpool Street thing, but there's just too many Old Bill and, like I say, Bill's a magnet.

Sometimes we get a police escort at South Tottenham but you can't rely on that. Other times their firm's seen us and not gone into us, mainly because there were too many Old Bill.

For the first game at the new Spurs stadium, there were at least 200 of us and we met after the game. We were obviously very happy being the first team to beat them at their new ground. At their new ground, away supporters can only come out one way, and we were walking down a road behind the ground.

The Old Bill were out in force that day; they were everywhere. Instead of turning right like they told us to, we turned left. That's when I saw Bill, and then blimey, we've only hit the High Street! Very quickly, Spurs come out from the pub opposite, a few with balaclavas on, to have a go.

A few of our lot went across to confront them. I got to the edge of the pavement, the horses turned up and it's all stopped. But it was just funny that the Old Bill, well, how can I put it? They were useless! They had no idea what to do. The Old Bill just got around us and ignored them. We pretty much had a copper each! They marched us back down the road and all round the houses to Seven Sisters station.

They wanted to keep us away from them, but obviously Spurs were in other places, waiting for us. To be fair, some of our younger ones were having verbals with them. I'm not sure if any punches were thrown, but as soon as the horses come along that was it, we couldn't do anything after that, even if we wanted to.

We were buzzing that day. Spurs may have not taken kindly to the banter, but who cares?

In the 80's, I wasn't with Bill all the time. I was with the ICF because they were the ones who would stand. Bill didn't have a lot of people with him, and he sort of drifted in and out of our company.

Me and Bill were together for about 10-15 years from the late 60's. After that I was with other people. But I'm always with him at Spurs.

The way I see it, I'm looking after a mate, one of my oldest mates. You can't always trust people at face value in the heat of the battle. Bill would probably say he'd be OK, but I'm never going to take that chance knowing how much he's despised over there.

Walking up Tottenham High Road you get in the ear all around you. "Gardner!" this and "Gardner!" that, and what they're going to do to him and us, and all that caper.

It's always the same, year in, year out. We get near the ground and all you ever hear is, "Gardner you wanker." I'm talking today, 100 percent today. They all know who Bill is over there.

Early Beginnings

I first met Bill when he was 14. I'm only a few years older than him myself.

I recall him standing his ground and ending up coming through what was a pretty heavy situation with a Chelsea scarf in his hand. He made an immediate impression, and I tapped him on the shoulder and just gave him a quick, "Well done, son!"

I think he wanted to be a part of something. Deep down, and I think he'll accept this, Bill was something of a loner. He wouldn't take orders from anyone and didn't seem to want to be a member of a firm. He'd knock about with us -The Teddy Bunter Firm (TBF) - and we'd travel to games together. But he was never really *in* the TBF. As far as I recall he wasn't into 'firms'.

He was his own man, but someone who any West Ham fan could turn to if they came unstuck. For determination, courage, and strength of character, I've met very few people like him. I suppose that's why he became a legend for so many West Ham supporters. He's Mr. West Ham, isn't he? But there's a lot more to Bill's character than people might read in a book, on a website, or see in a film. He's an incredibly funny man with a brilliant sense of humour.

Much like Bill, I've never accepted we were thugs. I've never considered myself, Bill, Bunter, or anyone who used to go to away games back then to be thugs.

Yes, we were a fiercely proud bunch, and as long as there was life in us, we'd defend West Ham's honour to the bitter end. As far as we were concerned that's precisely what we were doing.

I was at Hillsborough in 1964 to watch West Ham play Manchester United in the FA Cup semi-final. My mum made sure I was well turned out and put me in a suit that got completely ruined on the train journey up there, and soaked right through at the game.

Her dad was at the 1923 Cup final, and I was proud to follow the tradition. When people talk about the West Ham way there it is in a nutshell. Pride, honor, and tradition.

So, when rival supporters tried to stop us following those traditions, they can't honestly have thought we'd simply roll over.

We weren't brought up like that, and to do so would've been as far removed from the West Ham way as you could've got.

It meant we could sleep at night with a clear conscience, knowing we'd done right by our Club, our mates, and fellow Hammers.

Bill and Ted the Stewards

There's been a few bad decisions taken by the Club down the years, but one of the better ones was making Bill and me stewards for the old Irons Travel Club on those decrepit football special trains. Dennis Smith was the Club's man in charge back then, and he paid us to ensure there was no trouble on the journey to and from away games.

I suppose, in all honesty, I took my duties a little less seriously than Bill. I saw it as a great way to get paid to go to away matches and did precious little. Bill, on the other hand, wanted to earn his money.

So, while I was sat playing cards with the lads he'd walk up and down the train talking to people, making sure they were alright and nipping any trouble in the bud. That was his Mr West Ham side, and almost certainly the beginning of the affection and respect West Ham fans still have for him today. Today's fans were probably told about him by their fathers, and grandfathers.

I suppose if you want to try and pinpoint a time when that relationship between Bill and the fans began, that's as good a place to start as any. There was a flip side to it though.

As stewards, me and Bill had to wear special armbands. This made sure the Old Bill knew we were responsible for the safety of West Ham fans on those trains. But of course, when the shit hit the fan away from home, it had the potential to put us both in a rather compromising position!

One occasion I remember in the early seventies was arriving at Cardiff and, as per usual, ensured we kept tight and compact on the way to the ground.

In the absence of any police escort, this was the only way we could prepare to defend ourselves, because nine times out of ten we would be attacked by the home fans as soon as we left the station.

We'd make sure to keep those West Ham supporters who could look after themselves – which in fairness was the majority – close, and those who couldn't even closer. As usual, Bill was at the front of the group.

We left the station and began walking, as a group of around 50, towards the ground. I spotted a pub in the distance and I think it registered with Bill too. It looked quite run down, but there were a fair few people milling around outside. It was obvious they were our welcoming committee! Sure enough, the closer we got, the more locals started coming out to say hello.

Bill and I realised we were heading into the eye of the storm when it occurred to us it probably wouldn't go down too well in the Upton Park boardroom if two officially designated stewards who were there to prevent trouble, were caught bang in the middle of it. So off came the armbands before steaming into them. What were we supposed to do? We weren't going to miss the game and we weren't going to be intimidated. We also weren't very good runners!

Their lot were game; I'll give them that, but we more than held our own. When the Old Bill arrived, waving their truncheons about, our armbands went back on and both Bill and I told them we were official West Ham stewards and informed them how we had been attacked first.

I can still picture Bill remonstrating with these gormless Old Blll about how disgraceful the episode had been, and that he would be reporting the matter to the powers upon his return to London!

To be fair, I suppose that wasn't a particularly accurate account of events. But a night in a Welsh cell didn't particularly appeal to either of us and we were soon on our way; complete with a police escort.

I remember thinking thank goodness for those armbands, giving us that air of authority and the Old Bill swallowing everything Bill had to say, allowing us on our way with a police escort.

To many back then we were seen as a destructive social entity. But to those we cared about we were saviors. Going away to watch your team play a game of football was a million miles from what it's like today. There were some amazing characters back in those days, and Bill's personality made him someone many looked up to.

At that semi Hillsborough in '64, I was stood on the terraces mixing with thousands of Manchester United supporters. There was no trouble at all. Fast forward three years to West Ham against Manchester United at Upton Park and it was pandemonium.

I've often wondered what changed in those three years but have never been able to work it out. Nor do I really want to. At the end of the day, football went in a certain direction and you either stood or ran. From day one, and in my experience, West Ham never, ever ran. That's what made us special.

9

TRACED

St. Botolphs Cemetery,
Aldgate 1969

I was found in the graveyard by a copper one night. He was shining a torch and asked me what I was doing.
"What do you think I'm doing?" I replied. "I'm trying to get some kip."
I was taken to Bow Road Police Station and held there before a woman from the council came to see me. I was placed in care at a private home in Westmoreland Road, Hornchurch, with a foster parent; a woman, who was raking it in for doing fuck all.
There were two of us in there, me and another lad sharing a room. He told me one of the male helpers was noncing him. He'd take this young lad Morris dancing every Thursday night and abuse him. The lad would come home and I used to hear him crying in the middle of the night.
"What happened?" I'd ask.
"He did it to me again," he'd reply, sobbing.
"Don't worry mate, we'll soon be out of here?", I'd reply, not knowing if that was true He didn't talk a lot, but I'd hear him

some nights pissing his bed instead of going to the toilet because he was so frightened of going in the dark. I often wonder what happened to that fella. I hope he made it through, but I've got my doubts.

It was like an old hoarder's house, full of crap and I hated it there. I even told them about the young lad. The only way out of there was to go back home to my mum and dad's. "No chance," I thought.

A Visit from Mum

In the end I needn't have worried about it. They'd told my mum and dad I was in there a month earlier. They'd replied saying I was probably better off in there for the time being as they were having work done to the house. What a load of old bollocks that was!

My mum did eventually come round about a month after I'd been placed there. She said she was there to make peace. She told me to come home and that I'd proved my point. As soon as she walked into the room, I felt my weakness start to come back. 'Warrior Bill' was starting to fade away. "Maybe they've changed," I thought. I felt wanted by my parents for the first time in my life.

I gave it another go, but within a week it was back to how it was.

The rows, the fighting, the slaps, and the screaming started up. She was still shagging Uncle Ted, but they were rowing as well. My old man had started cooking for himself because she wouldn't make him anything for dinner. No one talked to each other and no one got on.

My dad didn't even think to ask me where I'd been for a year.

So I kept out of the way. I did my boxing and went out at night.

10

Bunter Marks

Bunter Marks who, with Big Ted, led West Ham's infamous TBF of the late '60s is a life-long friend of Bill's. They would travel to away games when the visiting support was numbered in the tens rather than thousands. Here Bunter recalls Bill's arrival on the scene at Upton Park, as well as outlining the origins of the TBF, and its place within the tapestry of Bill's terrace rise.

I was from East Ham, so West Ham was always going to be my club. My older brother started going before me, and then my uncle started taking us before I started going on my own. This would have been 1967 and I would have been sixteen.

I'd go with my mates from school, but I was soon making new mates up there. We started going boozing down the Queens and White Horse around Upton Park, and the Plough and Harrow in Leytonstone, places like that.

We ended up knocking around Stratford and Leytonstone where I met Ted, Simmo, Scobie, and all that lot who Bill used to knock about with. That's how we got together.

I was quite friendly with Bill by the late '60s. He was living in Forest Gate when he was married to his first wife. I used to go round to his, knock on his door, and we'd go out for a pint or something. We've been friends ever since. There wasn't much going on at that time. Other clubs were starting to have their own firms, but you wouldn't see them. There weren't any meet-ups because there weren't any mobiles.

We'd just bump into 'em, the other lot, after games. We'd have a fight in the street or something, but nothing too serious. It only really started getting proper nasty in the early '70s.

All the old boys talk about Manchester United at home in 1967. I was with the Baker Brothers, a little firm from the manor. There was another mob called the Arnie Garnie firm from Custom House who could look after themselves.

They were the main people in those days. Me and Simmo used to make out we was in with the Baker Brothers, and when it all went off in the north bank against Manchester United that night I thought, "Fucking hell, this is great!"

That's how it started for me. The Baker Brothers couldn't give a fuck in them days. They were at West Ham well before the Mile End Mob *or* the TBF.

When Bill used to come before the game, he went with anyone, but he wasn't into firms. Bill was Bill. He loved his football and he loved West Ham. He wanted to be on his own all the time, but he couldn't go to football on his own. Back then you'd have got murdered away from home. So he used to travel with us, everyone used to come with us all the time, but they often weren't members of our firm. That's all it was, mates. Then more people started going away and more people came with us, Bill included, and the firm started getting bigger. We weren't a big mob; we had about 50, sometimes 60 or 70. But it went from there and in time other firms came along, Canning Town, all that lot.

Some said there was a lot of friction between us and the Mile End, but there was no fighting between us, and when we used to go to away games we used to join up with them.

The name, the TBF, was my mate Simmo's idea. He said Mile End was named the 'Mile End Mob', and we should call ourselves the TBF after me and Ted. "What you talking about?" I said, but before long we were the TBF and everyone jumped on board.

We had an Asian fella, Singhy, who came from the manor and used to come to football. There was another fella, Carlos, who was Greek. We had everyone in our lot!

In them days you'd jump in the back of the old Transit and get as many as you could in there. You didn't know where you were fucking standing because there were no windows. When we got out the other end, they always knew we were from London, just by the way we dressed. West Ham weren't the only team with a firm.

Huddersfield, Stockport, you name them, they all had a firm, all wanting us off their manor. They had no chance with us. We went fucking everywhere. There were times it was only about 30 of us - the usuals - me, Ted, Bill, Scobie, and his brother, Lawrence, who we nicknamed Lol.

Huddersfield away in the cup was a lively one. That was the 71/72 season. We had a fight with their lot and then another one when a Leeds firm turned up.

Capital Punishment

London derbies became a bigger deal in those days. Word was spreading and more people were getting in on it. It was still easier getting from one side of London to the other than it was going up north, so all the London teams wanted to be top dogs.

The Harry Cripps testimonial comes to mind. That was quite interesting! Everyone turned out for that. Everyone. We met up with the Mile End lot, went into the Millwall end, and held it as long as we could.

For me, there were no winners that day. I'd say that both firms were evenly matched.

The Shed at Chelsea in the 72/73 season was a fucking war zone. Me and Bill both got nicked. We queued up and paid on the turnstile. There were no tickets or anything. No security, CCTV, police horses, nothing like that.

There were just a few coppers with truncheons. One of them warned me once, but I steamed in anyway when it all went off and ended up in Pentonville, after getting done for assault.

There were loads of us in the Shed that day, at least a couple of hundred West Ham just drifted in. Mile End was there, Canning Town was there, the TBF were there, Bill was there. Everyone showed up for that.

We used to do it all the time. We did it loads of times at Tottenham.

When the new lot were coming through, people like Cass, Carlton, Andy Swallow, they all looked up to me, Bill and Ted. Our lot were about the same age. Bill's a couple of years younger than me, Ted's a year older and Scobie's about my age.

The new lot were about five years younger than us. It ain't a lot now, but it's a bit of a gap when you're in your teens. They hung around with our lot and started travelling with us. They had a lot of respect for us all. They were good boys.

Bill the Man

Bill was himself. He wasn't with the TBF, he wasn't in the Mile End and he wasn't in the ICF. But we all accepted him, knew him, and respected him because he could have a proper tear-up like most of us. But with Bill, it was always out of love for the Club, for West Ham United.

I think that's probably why he didn't take to firms. He only ever saw one firm; the West Ham United firm.

That's probably why a lot of West Ham fans today, the ones who know our history, call him the Guvnor, Mr West Ham and all that. But he never thinks he's better or worse than anyone else. He was just his own man, that's all, and he loved the club to bits. I think he'd look at me funny if I started calling him the guvnor, so I might just do it next time I see him!

He was never scared to go in. The first in was always him and Ted. That's why I respect Bill, because he'd go to fucking Tottenham on his own if he had to. He looked after the Bobby Moore statue on his own when he heard Millwall was going to do it. That's the thing about Bill, he'll do things on his own if he has to, he isn't bothered.

He never bottled it. When the terraces were at their worst, he was always there. First up the fucking front. They'd all follow him or whoever was at the front at the time, the Cooper Brothers, Mile End, Ted, me, the Williams brothers or whoever.

But you'd always see Bill one of the first in. He never backed down. I've never known him to back down from a fight or get turned over.

You get these arseholes now who try and make a name for themselves by dropping his name in all the time. You know the ones, they've 'known Bill all his life, they know this, they know that'. They know fuck all. A bloke said to me once, "You know Bill Gardner?"

I said, "Yeah, why?"

He says, "I've known him fuckin years."

I said, "Well I don't know you. You never used to hang about with us." Why they do it I don't know. They can't make a name for themselves, so they make out they know him to get a bit of attention. They know fuck all. They like jumping on bandwagons, that's all.

It's like fucking stalking someone. A lot of people look up to us, that's fair enough. But don't tell me you're Bill's best mate because I've heard it all before.

For me, he's a gentleman. Every time I see him when I'm with the wife, he'll pull me to one side and say, "Bunt, if you got any money troubles, don't hesitate to phone me."

I think that's a mark of the man, still looking out for his mates after fifty-odd years. We might not have seen each other for months. But he never forgets, which is either a good thing or a bad thing depending on who you are and what you've done. To me, that's a great friend. I never have taken him up because I've got a family to borrow money from if I need to. But for him to come out and still be looking out for his mates is special.

Bill will always be like a brother. He's like family, a relation.

I think he felt he had to earn our respect. Well, he was right, he did have to earn it, everyone did. But fuck me did he come through it with flying colours! He earned our respect a million times over.

A gift from Charles Bronson for which
I'll be forever grateful

Working the doors

Early days

My fellow Hammer and good friend Roy

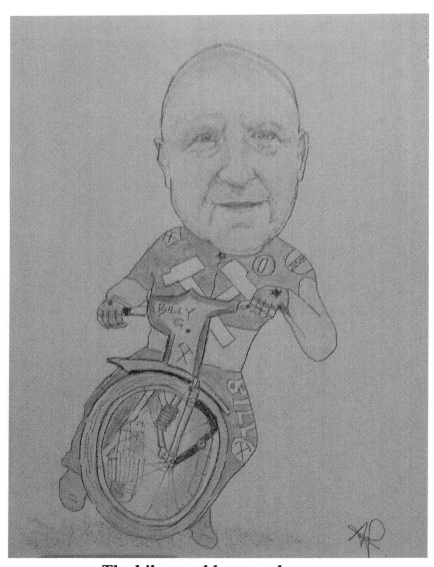

The bike would surrender now

A few of the Old Guard

The boys and their nan. A tough day for me

RIP Sir Bobby. Treated like shit by club and country

Me, Ted and my oldest boy James

Lol and Carlton

No thanks, done it before

John Lyall: A true West Ham gentleman

My soulmate, Sarah.

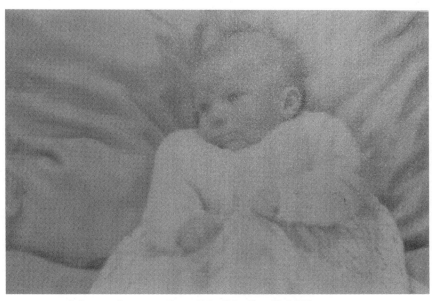

Me at 3 months old. Little did I know…

Proud of you boy. My Dan's graduation

Beware of snakes: They get everywhere

Bucharest 99

The boys never stood a chance!

Tbilisi. My left wrist don't half hurt!

Taking Red Square!

PART TWO

Acceptance

11

West Ham Beginnings

My first two games were Middlesbrough and Liverpool, the last two games of the 57-58 promotion season. My dad was a Spurs fan and had the cockerel on his pyjamas when he died. He started taking me to football when I was about seven - Tottenham one week, West Ham the next.

I used to watch the boys having a laugh at the back of the North Bank and think, "I wouldn't mind some of that." So I'd run up there They were all jumping up and down, having a laugh, having a bit of fun. Youngsters my age all went down the front and they'd pass me down above their heads. It was such a great atmosphere. I'd meet my dad afterwards and he never used to moan at me. He'd never tell my mum I'd gone missing either because she'd have stopped us going and he wanted to go to football as much as I did.

Tottenham had a great side. I saw them win the double playing some great football. They were a cut above any other London side. When I told him a few years later I didn't want to go to Tottenham anymore, it hurt him. He never said anything, but I know it did

Before '64 West Ham never won much, but I loved it there. You'd get off the train and people were milling around everywhere. There were little groups singing West Ham songs. The smell of the cafés years before the burger vans turned up, the noise from the heaving pubs and just the buzz about the place. There was a sense of real warmth and excitement.

You'll never get that kind of passion at this new ground, that's for sure. You'd go down to the ground and everyone was singing 'Bubbles'. The crowd used to sway, there'd be surges forward which would lift you off your feet. How no-one was ever killed is beyond me. There used to be so many people in there, most of them couldn't go to the toilet. Someone would say, "I want a piss", so you'd make a circle and they'd whip it out right there and then. You definitely wouldn't get away with at the new stadium! It was bloody horrible, but I can't help smiling about those days. That feeling of 24 or 25,000 people going home happy. Everyone was happy. You'd get on the train and they'd be doing 'Knees Up Mother Brown' holding onto those things on the tube that looked like a policeman's baton. That's when my old man stopped going football altogether, so I started going to West Ham on my own from about 11 years of age.

I used to get there at 9:30 in the morning on a match day. I'd be first in the queue, and I used to sit in the West Stand Upper, opposite the Chicken Run. I'd get Row A Seat 1, which meant I was looking down across the goal line. The North Bank was right next to me.

It was such a great sight. I had a fantastic view of the pitch and a better one of the North Bank. Those surges forward, the swaying, the noise, and the singing. It was amazing, just amazing. They looked incredible from up there. The pitch was like an electric green like someone had switched it on.

I met a bloke from Dagenham, an Irish fella who used to go and we'd take it in turns to get there first and keep each other's places in the queue. He'd say, "I'll get here next week at half past, you get there at 12:00." The doors would open at 12:30.

So, I'd be there one week queuing up for him and the next week it was vice versa. There was none of this bollocks of, "Oi, where you pushing in," it wasn't like that at all.

I bought my first season ticket in about 1968. It was a little book full of vouchers. I've stood all-round the ground, and enjoyed everywhere I'd been. I've loved meeting all the different people I've had the good fortune to. Different generations, fathers, sons, and grandchildren. They were all marvelous, marvelous people.

I only loved going over West Ham.

12

Acceptance

Ask any West Ham fan what attracted them to the Club? Nine times out of ten they'll say it was the football, where they were from, or winning the World Cup (you're welcome England). In my case, it was simply the fans.

For sheer camaraderie, pride, honour, passion, warmth, and a fearsome love of their own and their team, very few sets of fans matched West Ham's. I should know. I've met the rest.

Perhaps my circumstances made me more of a Hammer than others. When I had nothing but a few shopping bags and the belief that my life was of no value or consequence, those Saturday afternoons on the North Bank meant everything.

I loved West Ham, and the supporters. Being a loner, I used to wonder, "How will I be accepted here?" I craved friendship, respect, and self-worth. One of the earliest lessons I learned was that respect, friendship, and acceptance aren't just handed out on a plate.

They're things you have to earn. To get respect, you have to give it.

I've shown respect to every friend I've made, and I've shown resect to every enemy. It's a tough lesson to learn, but it'll stand you in good stead for all of the shit life throws at you.

In my case, it meant standing you're ground, of not running, picking your mate up off the floor, and never leaving anyone behind.

I wasn't going to be stepped on and I wasn't going to be bullied about by people with big mouths and bigger egos. It was about demonstrating honour and loyalty.

So, I stood my ground. It's as simple as that. That's how it started for me. But a leader? Leave it out. I was a boy for Christ's sake! I would just watch what some of the other blokes did when the fights started at Upton Park, and I did the same as them. I just stood my ground because I wanted them to accept me. I wanted them to like me.

The first battle I recall was Manchester United at home in 1967 when I was 13. Everyone knows about it. They had to win that game to win the league, but ended up beating us 6-1. They had fans everywhere around Upton Park that night, most of them from London. There were thousands of them and, to be fair, they murdered us on the night.

It was brutal. There were bottles and all sorts flying about and there was claret everywhere. We gave them a run for their money as some fans on both sides ran to escape it all.

I just stood there; watching it go off rooted to the spot. It was fascinating, in a strange sort of way. There was so much anger in that stand. But I wasn't scared. That's not me boasting. Looking back, I should've been. I made the decision there and then which would define the rest of my life, and steamed in for the first time.

I took a slap; I took more than a few slaps. But I gave back a fair few, and more. I didn't go down and kept moving forward. It was carnage and I don't know if anyone saw me having it with them.

If I'm being truthful, I wanted them to see me. I wanted the West Ham fans to know that I wasn't a runner; that I wasn't a coward, that I would fight alongside them until the bitter end. To accept me as one of their own.

I don't think anyone did see me that night. It's not like I pulled up any trees or anything. But on the way home I felt I'd done my bit. I hadn't run, I'd stood my ground and shown no fear. For the first time in a very long time – perhaps ever – I felt good about myself. I wasn't that scared little boy who'd sat crying under the table when his mum and dad were going at it. I wasn't fearful of the pain of getting a clump. It brought back memories, but they spurred me on. I didn't set out to be anything bigger, better or different to any of the other West Ham fans who defended the Club's honour that night. I never have. We were all in it together.

I started to make friends and began to feel popular which I'd never felt before. After the Saturday game, and after I'd left home, I'd go back to my cemetary and revert to being anonymous.

I'd spend one week reliving the previous Saturday, and the second building up to the next. I'd immerse myself in books and taught myself to read and write.

But at the back of my mind, it was, "West Ham, West Ham, West Ham…"

I never confided in my new friends about being homeless. Why would I? The whole point of creating a new 'me' was blocking out the old one. That meant not talking about it.

I can see that now, but couldn't back then. I've spent most of my life blocking out those early years, and the effect they had.

In any case, I could never tell my new mates where I was living. For one thing, they'd never had believed me and, for another, I didn't want to be around people outside of football.

I was still only a kid and, although I could feel parts of my personality changing, deep down I was still pretty vulnerable and suspicious of people's motives and actions.

I was still living on a knife-edge.

13

Peterborough Tony

British serviceman Corporal 'Peterborough Tony' was engaged in a frenetic firefight with Serb nationalists in the early '90s. He was in Bosnia monitoring Serb warlord Arkan and his entourage's movements.

At the height of carnage, Tony stopped firing and looked at his troops around him. They were petrified, which prompted a sense of guilt. These were his troops. He was their CO. They looked up to him.

At the grim height of reality, a voice from the past kicked its way into Tony's consciousness from the terraces of three decades earlier.

"Hold your ground, hold your ground! Forward, forward, forward."

"They were Bill's words," Tony tells me. "They were just Bill's words in my head."

"Despite our friendship, I don't think Bill's ever really been aware of how much he has influenced my life. I wouldn't be half the man I am if I hadn't first met him as an impressionable youngster many years ago.

"The two situations seem miles apart – war and fighting on the terraces - but the primal instincts are the same. Fight or flight. The emotions are the same. Bill led from the front. Always. No-one left behind, all getting back in one piece. Thankfully, we did.

"In the '70s and early '80s, West Ham's firm was a bit like a regiment. For me, Bill was our leader, the one we followed, the one we knew we could rely on. But our strength was our unity.

"He would have been brilliant in the forces, as a senior officer. His unit would have followed him everywhere and anywhere, the way many of us did back then.

"There are good people, and there are bad people who get rank in the forces. Bill would have been one of the top ones. I can say that through my 15 years of experience, because of his calm demeanor and positivity in the face of adversity.

"Bill taught me a valuable lesson all those years ago. He taught me that fear is infectious. Show any sign of weakness at the height of the battle and it'll spread among your men.

"Don't get me wrong, it's scary getting shot at. It's scary when the fucking grenades are going off. It's scary when you're getting mortared. But fear is infectious.

"So, you have to stamp it out. It doesn't matter if you've got a rifle in your hands or empty fists. It's a primal human instinct. The best way to stamp out fear is by staying calm during the chaos.

"You always felt safe whenever you heard Bill had arrived at an away game. He was a big man and calm as fuck. That's how I always saw him. I still picture him now leading from the front: "Don't worry, lads, don't worry. We'll sort this out, we'll be alright. Them mugs ain't got the bollocks. Never have, never will."

"It's all well and good talking about it. But Bill was on the coalface, always on the front-line. Always. I grew up worshipping him. I saw him at my first game at Upton Park. My uncle took me and whispered in my ear, "That's him, that's Bill Gardner," before returning to his pre-game pint in the Boleyn. I used to see him at away games. It was like seeing a God when I was only a sprog, a nervous little kid. I was only 12, but I remember feeling starstruck. His name was getting mentioned more and more at the club, and my uncle kept me fully briefed.

"By my late teens, I'd joined the terrace movement and when it kicked off, Bill would be the first man I'd look to for leadership. Me and many others. To be honest, he's still got that pop star quality for me, and I'm 60! That awestruck child who first saw him is no longer a child, but I'm still in awe at what he's done for me. He's had a massive influence on my life.

"That influence carries on like a wave. There are people who I've hopefully influenced in the forces because I was thought of as a strong character. Thing is, a lot of that character was instilled in me by Bill.

"So, hopefully, some of the young recruits I've worked with have said, "I want to be like him." If I've inspired any of them about bravery, courage, and honour, that's just Bill speaking through me.

"I work with recruits and they always talk about their corporals as being tough, hard men. So, there'll be young lads now, serving with that dedication and respect, who I would've worked with. The values they have, whether it be in Afghan, Kuwait, wherever, will be the ones Bill instilled in me. Through me, from Bill.

"For someone with such a huge reputation, it's amazing how few people really know Bill the man. Loads of blokes claim to, and it's almost always two things - either they've done him or he's their best mate!

"In fairness, it only winds me up now if it's the latter. If everyone who claims to have done Bill has done, they're either bullshitting or didn't do a very good job. I've genuinely never seen Bill turned over or take a backwards step at football.

"Bill practices what he preaches. He respects others and will always pose for photographs for any West Ham supporters. It doesn't matter what he's doing, he's always got the time for West Ham fans, he's always polite.

"He accommodates people, so he's probably had his photo taken more times than Princess Di did!

"I remember a bloke showing me a photo of him and Bill. "That's me and me mate Bill Gardner," he said. "Fuck off mate," I thought.

World Cup, Spain 1982

"That's probably when I went from being an acquaintance to a mate of Bill's. I bumped into him at an England game and he told me he remembered me - that made me feel 10 feet tall. West Ham used to go quite mob-handed to England games, but in fairness to Bill he was never interested in the England scene.

"He's West Ham first, always, forever - true claret and blue. Apart from the World Cup in Spain in 1982, I don't remember seeing Bill at many England games. He was probably waiting for the next West Ham pre-season friendly in Europe or China or America!

"With England, we had the reputation, but I shudder to think what we would have been like with Bill leading us. That would've been incredible; uniting all the rival firms like Derby and Leeds.

"They weren't the only two rival firms who'd play-up at England games, the Bristol clubs hate each other, same with the Sheffield boys. Bill would have sorted that right out, just like he did when he united the firms at West Ham to make us the best there was. With England, us West Ham used to pretty much keep to ourselves. At one game I remember thinking we've probably mugged off all this lot at one point or another; I don't think we've made many friends!

In fairness, it worked out best for everyone because when it went off, West Ham were usually first up the front, but we'd always stick together as a firm.

Becoming a Hammer

I'm not from the manor and my accent gives that away, so I get asked about supporting West Ham a lot.

For me it goes back to 1966. We had a TV at a time when many people didn't. I invited a load of my friends round and the fucking thing broke down!

I cried my eyes out so my mum said, "I'll take you to the pictures and we'll watch it in colour." I remember it clear as day. We were right down the front and the players looked massive. And it was in colour, which was unbelievable! They played an Alf Garnett film before the game. I can't remember what the film was, but he was West Ham wasn't he?

So, he's West Ham and along comes the World Cup, and all I'm hearing is, "It's Bobby Moore of West Ham over here and it's Geoff Hurst of West Ham over there, Martin Peters of West Ham try's his luck."

I thought, "Blimey, that West Ham team don't sound half bad." The seed had been planted. I didn't know it at that stage, but the older I got the more I watched out for their games on *Match of the Day* and started checking West Ham's results. By the time I was 11 I was obsessed. I was officially a Hammer.

I daresay the World Cup did the same for a few others. I couldn't go to a game for a long time, but that's what did it for me.

There's something special about being a West Ham fan, and it's not just special needs! There's something very special about following this club because it's a special club to follow. It's hard to put into words, but I'll have a go. It's a family without a doubt, and very much like a regiment. We look after each other, and we look after the one's who are less able to. Those values were instilled in me by Bill. I suppose I was destined to serve in a regiment whose colours were claret and blue. I'd rather not say which regiment that was, if it's all the same.

Bosnia, 1990s

Tony was awarded the Commendation for Bravery by Her Majesty the Queen after saving the lives of three British soldiers in Bosnia. His pride was however tainted after witnessing a war atrocity.

He freely admits returning home a different person to the one who departed the UK to serve his country abroad.

"The three servicemen veered off the side of a mountain. I got them out. They were all injured, and I believe lost their careers. One was garroted by his own webbing and I got him out.

"I tried dragging the other two away but couldn't move them too far. In the end, I disengaged the engine and made the vehicle safe. Fortunately, it didn't go up.

"But the war crime was the worst. That was tough. We were monitoring Arkan, which put us up against Arkan's Tigers. I looked him straight in the eye. I stared at him from 2 feet away. I was big in those days and he just looked at me like a piece of shit.

"We were watching where he was staying. He walked straight past, and I just fucking stood there and stared at him and he fucking stared back at me, staring down his nose at me.

"His lot killed an eight-year-old girl and I witnessed that. That's all I'll say about it but, to be honest, it's something I've found difficult to deal with.

"I'd come back from Bosnia and was at a pretty low ebb, to put it mildly. Bill called me to see how I was. During the conversation, he called me a hero.

"I can't put into words the impact those words coming from Bill had on me. Bill Gardner calling me a hero!

"I was grateful to him. It made it a lot easier and helped me get through some tough times.

"It's a chapter I've tried to put well behind me. As to why Bill is one of the very few people I've confided in, I honestly don't know. I suppose it comes down to who you trust. Speaking for myself, I'd trust Bill Gardner with my life."

14

Me, the ICF, and the Truth

"It's one of the things I can never get my head around," Bill tells me. "Everyone assumes I was the leader of the ICF.

"It don't make me angry, but it does make me laugh, because it's a load of bollocks. That much came out in court back in 1987.

"I was never a member of the ICF, let alone their leader. We moved in completely different circles.

"They were younger than me, did their own thing, and, with no disrespect, they were never a patch on the Mile End Mob.

"Don't get me wrong, I had, and still have, good mates who were in the ICF. But I never followed them. I never followed anybody

"Without sounding big-headed, it was more the other way around. There were times I helped a few of them out when it was all getting on top, and I was glad to.

"They were West Ham, that's all that mattered. But I never needed the ICF. I never needed anyone.

"It did used to make me laugh when around 300 West Ham fans would give it the ICF chant, especially away, and you'd have a look at them and there were only around 20 proper members in the group.

"I never followed them for one simple reason – I've never followed anyone in my life. That's my character. Some people have described me as a loner. That's not strictly true, but I was hiding a secret and sometimes found that easier to do than others.

"I was never into gangs. I never felt the need to rely on the help of others. I relied on myself – as I'd had to for many years as a kid - my values, my self-belief and the love of my team.

West Ham was a family to me, a real family, and that's how I treated West Ham supporters, gang or no gang.

"If you were West Ham and in trouble, you'd have my backing 110 per-cent.

People started to cotton on to that, and perhaps that's where the reputation came from.

And while was never something I went looking for, it was a responsibility I'd refuse to shirk."

The ICF were alright. I got on alright with them and they had some good lads. They weren't for me because they were younger. Like someone's said he's 55, I'm 64, but a nine-year gap in a group of lads is a big difference.

They did have a lot of hangers-on in my opinion. Away from home they'd start singing "ICF" and there'd be a load of muppets joining in with them who didn't even know them. That I didn't like a lot. But on the whole they was a good bunch of lads. A lot of them have grown up now, all in their 50's or older, and I'm still mates with loads of them.

But I was a different generation. It was like the Teddy Boys, Rockers, Suedeheads, Mods and Skinheads. All different generations. My generation was the Skinhead scene. The ICF's generation was like the next lot down the line, the next lot off the

West Ham conveyer belt. They were more like the first Casuals, always worried about their appearance, always well dressed. With me it was completely different. Looking back now I always used to look like a sack of shit compared to them! But in fairness I went there to do a job of work and didn't want to get dressed up in my best gear and chance ripping it. If you're going to go and dig the garden don't do it with your best clothes on. I used to have a donkey jacket, boiler suit, Doctor Martins...just normal clothes I suppose. Mind you I did have an orange boiler-suit. I must of looked like a right cunt in that. For me it was always the love of the club first, but if we could get a row at the end of it that'd make it a Brucie bonus.

I had my own people, and we didn't have a name. There was none of this gang and that gang, or which one was harder. We just went to the games. A lot of them said Bill Gardner's gang. A lot of them said we were part of the Teddy/Bunter firm. That was never the case. We mixed in more with the Teddy/Bunter firm than the ICF, but that was because I'd known them longer and the ICF were the new kids on the block, and they showed us respect. But we knew each other, and when the shit hit the fan we were all in it together, the West Ham United firm, which was all I ever wanted – unity. That's all I've ever wanted since I was a kid.

15

West Ham... United?

The height of the acrimony over the ill-fated anti-GSB march in 2018 brought back painful memories of a time when West Ham's supporters were far from united.

"Each West Ham firm has its manor, which they defended to the hilt. I've always termed it *the District line derbies* after the underground line, which took you to Upton Park. I suppose you could say they were West Ham firms from particular stops along the line. Very few outsiders used to get in. You wouldn't get into the Barking firm, or the Elm Park firm, or the Plaistow firm unless you were from there and supported West Ham. Unfortunately, it took tribalism to new heights at home games – and sometimes away from football. It was more than I could stomach.

"It was a bad time to be a West Ham fan and reminds me of a problem Millwall never got to grips with – uniting the fans. Their firms are still kicking the shit out of each other when there's no one else to fight. And then they boast they'd never write a book. Well that's hardly surprising – who'd have the bollocks to!?

It would go off every Saturday at West Ham in the early to mid-70's. Barking West Ham would wait at Barking station for the trains to pull in to have a row. Southend West Ham, Romford West Ham and Basildon West Ham would get off and Barking would be waiting for them. It was open season and we're talking 50-a-side fights with big blokes kicking the shit out of each other on the station platform. It was horrible, and many people will tell you that. Little firms like Basildon would be fighting for their lives.

"Mile End and Barking West Ham used to have some proper tear ups. Barking was quite a big firm – never a patch on Mile End – but they were all game. They had some really good lads, some good boys who could have a row. Ross Collier came from Barking and he was proper tasty. He was up there with the top five of all time in my eyes. He was a lot older than me and a proper geezer. After one evening game at Upton Park in the mid-70s, it went right off in the middle of Green Street between Barking and Mile End. The Teddy Bunter firm was in with the Barking boys, and they were having it with Mile End. So, I got in the middle and said, "For fuck's sake, enough's enough. If we keep on like this we're gonna get nowhere. If we join together we could be the best. You're all my mates, so why should I fight any of you. Let's go as one group." I didn't know some of the Barking lads, but enough of the main faces to be able to knock all that bollocks on the head.

"I had friends in all groups. They didn't want to row with me, and I didn't want to row with them, and they saw sense. It's as simple as that. They saw the light and agreed, "We ain't gonna do this, we're gonna stick together." I just said to a few of my mates, "We won't get anywhere if we carry on like that." A lot of

West Ham fans disappeared after that. Some didn't agree with it, which I understand. But most saw it as the way forward, because it was.

"It didn't stop instantly, but it got less and less. I think people were still wary of Mile End – everyone was wary of Mile End – but it got better and better to the point where all of a sudden, we were one. Mile End went with it some of the way, but not all the way.

"I stopped it, and people will tell you I stopped it. Life changed a lot. It got a lot easier for everybody. Nobody used to worry about getting off the trains where there'd be another West Ham mob waiting to fill them in. Everyone got used to being unified.

After that, Canning Town and Stratford West Ham were at it for a bit but that soon got sorted. Like everything in life, you can only do so much. Ultimately, people have got to decide what side they're on. Fortunately, both saw sense, and things went back to normal. On the whole, after it all got sorted, we were unified and that was our strength. We used to say we'll never leave a man down. Never. Ever. If you were ever caught leaving a man down words would be had.

That unity was sort of the birth of the ICF in spirit, if not body. The Persil tickets gave it a body. The ICF looked after each other and took that unity towards fellow West Ham fans seriously, which I liked.

It carried on like that for a good few years, but over the last five years certain aspects of it have started to creep back in. The white powder also changed it a bit, when people started putting drugs and money before loyalty. Greed got in the way and some West Ham firms were competing for territory. The animosity started up a bit, but it's not reached the levels it used to. Having said that, I've seen signs that it could do.

16

Frank McAvennie

I was very much a fan before becoming a professional footballer, which I got into quite late. I used to follow Celtic home and away, which would mean a lot of pub and terrace talk. There was a lot of talk about the state of the game down there in England with all terrace agro.

As a fan, I'd heard of Bill. Following Celtic to away games you'd talk to other supporters who'd been down to England. We knew all about the trouble happening down there.

West Ham fans had quite a reputation, as did other clubs like Millwall and Chelsea. Scotland had its own problems, but that was very much about Celtic and Rangers. But I knew about the West Ham – Millwall rivalry even before signing for West Ham.

When I joined, quite a few of the players either knew or knew of Bill, particularly the ones from the area. Tony Cottee used to travel to away games as a kid with his dad before turning pro.

He naturally met a few of the boys travelling to away games and told me Bill was a very highly respected figure among the fanbase. "Mr West Ham," he called him.

TC told me he was accused of grassing Bill up at an away game at Birmingham a few years earlier. He was fuming! TC was – and still is – a West Ham fan. He said the idea he could've done that made him sick, but that fortunately Bill had set the record straight. I'm stood there talking to Tony Cottee, nodding away, and all the while I'm thinking, "Fuck me, who is this Bill Gardner fella!"

Frank and Bill

For those of us players who liked a night out on the town, the ICF boys looked after us superbly. People like Cass, Carlton, Swallow - they were great to me. They were good people whose company I enjoyed. The ICF boys looked after me on more than a few occasions, and we had some great nights.

You'd never see Bill out on the town after a game though. It never seemed his thing. But the boys used to speak so highly of him. They respected him massively and sort of looked up to him.

The Chadwell Heath 'Groundsman'

I remember speaking to a groundsman at Chadwell Heath in the 1986-87 pre-season. It's fair to say the players were on a huge downer, after coming third and just missing out on the league title for the first time in the club's history on the last weekend of the season.

This bloke told me he'd only let himself believe we had a chance of the league after a mesmerising Easter bank holiday, when we beat Chelsea 4-0 at the Bridge, before seeing off Spurs 2-1 on Easter Monday at Upton Park.

A lot of the supporters I spoke to at the time still didn't think we were in with a chance of taking the league title to the final weekend. But with the run we were on, and the two fixtures coming up (Chelsea and Spurs), many West Ham fans were saying to me, "Beat them two and it's been a brilliant season!"

"You alright?" I asked the groundsman at Chadwell Heath.

"Yeah," he said, with that pained but dignified look so common to West Ham supporters. "To be fair, we normally come down with the Christmas decorations," he added.

"You lot didn't," he said. "You fought to the bitter end. You fought against the weather, playing three games a week in the run-in. You kept us on the edge of our seats for the whole season."

"You fought for each other and you played as a team, and you earned the right to play some of the best football I've seen us play. You made me proud."

I looked the bloke up and down. He was huge.

I noticed a tattoo on one of his forearms. They were like tree trunks. The tattoo read, "Bill Gardner".

It turned out I was talking to Bill I was talking to Bill and hadn't even realised it. The man I'd heard so much about! It was strange finally meeting him in the flesh after everything I'd heard about him as a kid on the terraces, and now as a West Ham player.

It hurt him, that season. You could see that. After all those years supporting the club, to have come so close. West Ham had never come closer. They never have since. I could see it in his face like he was wondering if he'd ever see us go that close again.

It's sad because those fans are special. They deserve success.

No one was to know that Bill and a few of the boys would soon be having their own fight in the courts. But at that moment, with him at Chadwell Heath, I just saw a die-hard fan who'd seen his team come so close to the ultimate prize, only to have it snatched away at the final hurdle. He was hurting. As a fan, I completely understood that.

I don't know why that memory has stayed with me all these years. Bill has an amazing presence. It's not just because he's a big fucking bloke. There's an air to him, which for me encapsulates West Ham values – dignity, pride, passion.

He speaks with the conviction of a man who sees this club as a huge part of his life, with his heart on his sleeve and claret and blue blood in his veins.

Arriving a Player – Leaving a Son.

When West Ham reached their peak, even I knew, as a Scotsman, that the boys at West Ham won the World Cup for England. Your Martin Peters, your Geoff Hurst's, and your Bobby Moore's. What great players. What a great global advert for the club. That part of London may have its problems – much like the East End of Glasgow – but fuck me they could produce some players!

So, there was no question of me not wanting to go to West Ham when I found out they had contacted St. Mirren about me.

I was an attacking midfielder and was being brought in to support Tony and Paul Goddard upfront.

I knew the fanbase was enormous, but it wasn't about that. I went there because of the way they played their football. They did everything right. They played the game the way I wanted to play the game. They got the ball down and wanted to play with some flair.

For me, as a player, that was ideal. There were other moves open to me, other clubs with their own styles of play. But West Ham wanted to play the ball out from the back, a style that suited me completely. There was a clear philosophy of the way they wanted to play, they got the ball down and played from the back. When I went to West Ham that was imprinted in the club's DNA.

John Lyall was a great man when it came to providing a football education. He had a totally different way of looking at football.

When I went there for my first pre-season, I thought they were taking the piss to be honest with you. They got the ball out! In Scotland, you didn't see the ball for two weeks in pre-season. You didn't get near a ball. It was all about the running, in the gym, doing weights, you know, just getting rid of all the weight you'd put on over the summer. But John was all about technical ability on the ball, which he'd learned from the great Ron Greenwood.

Like I've said, the fans there were great to me at West Ham. They still are! I think that comes back to being a fan first and player second. I fed off them and left everything on the pitch, and they fed off that. It was a two-way thing.

A Spoilt Dinner Date

I was out having a meal with my girlfriend on one occasion, at a pub not far from Chadwell Heath, where a Spurs fan was giving me a load of shit. I told him to leave it out a couple of times, but he kept on.

I went to the toilet, deciding whether to fuck off somewhere else or shut the bloke up. I walked out of the bathroom into the dining area and I looked over towards him. He wasn't there.

As I walked around the bar, I could see his trainers, then jeans, then blood-stained t-shirt. He was ok, we could hear him swearing.

Around him, there were a couple of small cards.

"Congratulations, You Have Just Met The ICF," they read. I'm not condoning it, but it happened, so it's pointless pretending it didn't. And it made me laugh. Like I said, the boys looked after me down there.

1985-86

After pushing Liverpool and Everton to the final weekend of the season, the players were naturally gutted. The situation with the weather made it worse, with us having to play so many rearranged games in the run in.

But when I look back on it now, when I think of that first season at West Ham, the main memory I get is how much I enjoyed playing football for that team.

I won trophies and titles with Celtic and have played for my country in some big games. But that season, '85-86, I've never enjoyed playing football so much before or since. We played with the freedom John gave us. We played like mates down the park. I'll never forget that time of my life.

We played some top, top football and I enjoyed every single minute of it. No big-heads, no egos – John Lyall made sure of that – but a great team.

I was away on Scotland duty the following season and Kenny Dalglish, who had been my idol as a kid, told me we were the best team in the League that season. That meant a hell of a lot to me. When the player-manager of the Champions and the man who scored the goal at Stamford Bridge to win that Championship tells you it should have been West Ham, you know you've done something right.

It wasn't all sweetness and light of course. After losing Paul for the season on the opening day at Birmingham I was moved up front, Alan Dickens came in to replace me, and the rest is history.

That can't have been easy for Paul. He was some player, some goal-scorer. As a professional, I was asked to fill his role and we went on an amazing run. But as a human being, I always thought, "Fuck me, this will be hard for Paul." In fairness, Paul was a great pro and took it in his stride.

After six or seven games we were doing OK, but we thought we could do better. So, the players called a meeting. No manager or coaches, just the players.

The upshot of that was that TC was told in no uncertain terms he'd have to track back. Tony's the best natural goal-scorer I've played alongside. It's all he wanted to do and he was brilliant at it. But fuck me what a goal-hanger!

In all seriousness, I think he knows it made him a better player, and we kicked on from there.

A Telling Off at Orient

It was pre-season 1985, and we'd had a poor first half. As I was walking across the pitch towards the tunnel, I could see John remonstrating with a bloke. I walked past and into the dressing room.

I was knackered! Just then, John walked into the dressing room with the biggest guy I've ever seen stood next to him. There wasn't much of him that didn't have a tattoo on, and quite a few were West Ham. He was still shouting at John.

"They're a fucking bunch of overpaid cunts, they're dog-shit, my boy could do better than this lot. Cunts, cunts the lot of them!"

Silence. No one said a fucking word. We just looked at John.

"Don't tell me, tell them!" he yelled back at the bloke before leaving the dressing room. That was all the motivation I needed and mysteriously found my second wind the second half The guy was still seething as he was led away.

The Chicken Run & Me

I loved the Chicken Run to bits, and they seemed happy with the effort I was putting in. For an away full-back or winger, I can only think they dreaded playing at Upton Park.

One of them was Alan McDonagh, God rest his soul. He was giving TC an awful kicking in the first home game of the 85-86 season. I yelled out to Tony to switch sides.

"What you doing here?" Alan asked me. "You'll get the same as your mate."

"Come with me," I shouted back as I made a run towards the Chicken Run. He followed me, and as the ball went out of play, I put the brakes on.

Alan sped past me not having time to stop, and ended up in the Chicken Run. The fans started jumping all over him. I ran away into the box with a grin on my face. When he caught up with me, he gave me dogs abuse.

"What you doing? They're fucking punching me in there man!" I can't condone punching players. But I also can't deny how funny it was!

17

Leaving Upton Park

I never go back to look at what's there now. I can't do it. That last night when I left, I walked for hours afterwards; I didn't want the night to end, because I knew it was the end. It was a hard one. Looking back, perhaps I should have called it a day then, like so many of my good friends who refused to go to Stratford. I went into the toilet after the game and half closed the door. I sat on the khasi because I wanted to be the last one out. I thought, "Well if I hang on here the stewards are going to move me on," so I waited until they came round and checked the toilets. I thought if I close the door, they'll know someone's in there, have it half-closed. I was really quiet, which is hard for me. I knew the steward, and when he pushed the door open and said, "Come on Bill, it's time to go." I just said, "OK mate." I was in there a good 20 minutes after the last West Ham fan had gone; a good 20 minutes. When I come out there was no one there, no one.

I got out, walked round to the Boleyn, there were about seven or eight people there. I decided to walk to Canning Town. I don't know why. Like I say, I didn't want the night to end. I got a cab to Victoria and there were no trains. There was something wrong with the Gatwick Express. There were a couple of West Ham fans. I saw a man and his wife and they were going to

Horley, which is further on than me, so we ended up splitting the cab fare. My share was 70 quid. I got home at about 4-4.30 in the morning.

That night was emotionally draining for me, because when I had nothing that shithole was my home. That was my home and they were my people. It's the hardest thing I've ever done, and the worst I've ever felt. I felt despair, I felt lonely; I felt like that kid again. It was a pain I've never felt before When my mum and dad died I never felt that pain. I just felt like somebody took everything away.

I felt a lot of pain that night. It's not one of these things where people say, "Come on, get over it, it's gone now we got this nice new stadium." Not for me.

It isn't only personal to me, I'm one of many. But I felt it deeply. There hasn't been a day go by I haven't shed a tear over it, my Sarah will tell you that. I never knew what a broken heart was until that. I can't explain it. People will probably think I'm being way over the top, thinking, "Oh yeah, he's hurt, he must've split up with his bird, or lost someone close to him." But it wasn't like that. I've suffered all that and then some. Leaving Upton Park was worse. I've never suffered the hurt that caused me, never. I was a fucking wreck. I loved that place more than they'll ever know.

18

Gary 'Boatsy' Clark (Nottingham Forest FC)

I think Bill was getting out of the terrace movement just as I was getting into it, but yeah, our paths did cross back in the day. I can just remember him being this massive presence.

I've been a Forest supporter as long as I can remember, as a kid back in the seventies before getting into the casuals' scene in the early '80s.

I followed Forest everywhere, and by the time I left school, I threw myself into the Casuals culture. The music, the clothes, and eventually the football.

I ended up making a name for myself on the terraces, I guess, at least that's what I get told. But that's a long time ago now, and those days are over. We've moved on to different things and, now and then, I'll meet up with a few of the boys at West Ham.

Cass has always been a good mate. It's funny in a way, I guess. We all used to try and batter each other senseless on a Saturday back in the '70s and '80s, but a few of us are good mates now.

I first heard of Bill from the old lads at Forest, obviously one or two knew who all the top boys were at the time and I just used to hear his name all the time. When I left school and I started going to football with the boys about '81, West Ham were the top dogs, no doubt.

Bill's name was regularly heard in the pubs. It was "West Ham this, West Ham that, oh yeah and they've got this lad called Gardner, supposed to be a bit tasty."

What I like about Bill is he's always got a good word about Forest. I think he came up here when he was a kid, about 15-16, and he's talked about coming to Nottingham and getting looked after by the Forest Green Boat Mob of the '70s. He speaks fondly of Forest, which I obviously appreciate.

The casual scene and the terrace movement went hand in hand, and West Ham had the reputation. They had the numbers, and they had Bill Gardner. The word was he was their leader.

The name 'Bill Gardner' was legendary back then. If you knew the right people at football, especially the older ones, he was the one they'd talk about.

We've always been football fans. Just like Bill, he's always been a fan. He loves the game; I know he keeps an eye on young players coming through at West Ham.

When they come to Forest, we take them into the hospitality section. It's mad I suppose. We're all similar people from sillier backgrounds, aren't we? We love football, and we like a drink.

But we've all moved on.

When Forest went to West Ham in the late '70s, we had a good firm to be fair. It was just before my time, but I used to see the trouble from a distance.

Forest were in the old 2nd Division so we didn't play West Ham for a few years. But on this occasion Forest went down to London thinking they were going to turn them over, thinking they were top dogs or whatever and they got a bit of a surprise at West Ham.

It didn't last very long because they were halfway back up the M1 before the game even kicked-off. They got chased out of the end, chased out of the ground, and chased out of London.

In the early 80's West Ham came to Nottingham in the league. It all went off that night. Forest got run ragged all over Nottingham that night.

The first time I saw Bill was around '82. The previous three times West Ham had come to Forest they just took the place.

We'd gathered at Nottingham station and a copper said, "They're at Leicester, if you fuck off home you better get gone now because they're all coming." I can remember it was about 1 o'clock and we were all in the King George pub facing the old bus station and got word West Ham had come off the train and were coming up the road. It was a bit of a hill; there used to be a sports shop on the corner and they just spread out in the middle of the road. There was probably only about 50 of them. To us, they just looked like massive fucking blokes. Forest scattered everywhere and I remember I nearly got knocked over by a double-decker bus.

I can always remember Bill; he was in the middle of them. None of them ran or anything, they didn't say anything, they just walked along towards Forest. Bill had a long duffle coat on with long curly blonde hair, he stood out a mile at the front. We're looking to all our older lads thinking, "What's going on here, we've all just disintegrated."

I must admit, he looked a frightening presence. I don't think I was going to do much against him, put it that way! I don't think too many fancied having it with him. We looked up to our elders, those who were 4-5 years older than us, but West Ham were proper men; it was men against boys.

About two years later they came again. I was at Her Majesty's doing a few months, and Forest played West Ham at home. My mates came to visit me, and told me West Ham came up again with a firm of around 60-70. But Forest had a major firm out that day; it must have been about 300-strong.

Bill led them over the bridge and they got ambushed across the other side. There was a derelict building nearby, and Forest managed to get a load of bricks from everywhere and waited for them. Bill spotted it and got his boys against some advertising hoardings, which had been moved from the nearby shops. That's when Forest started hitting them with bricks and Bill walked across the road to face them.

Everyone up here says if it wasn't for Bill that lot would've been killed. He just got them together with their backs against the wall apparently and the Old Bill came in with horses and truncheons; but he held it together. Forest were out for revenge and bricks were just raining down of them.

So, his credibility went up 110 percent in Forest's eyes, and he had a big reputation anyway.

Unique Time?

Yeah, without a doubt. If you were a football fan and you didn't fight, you couldn't go to away games.

It wasn't just the trouble, it was everything that went along with it. The clothes, the music, the football, the camaraderie; meeting your mates on a Saturday and defending your town. It was the whole weekend. It was exactly the same with the mods and rockers and the skins and punks who'd gone before us.

Fighting has been part of British culture long before football came along. I'm not glorifying it but I wouldn't change it for anything. I had a great time and met some great people.

You'll never be able to recreate the environment of that time today.

CCTV killed it in the end. You don't even have to throw a punch to get arrested 3 months later, after your doors have been put through by the Old Bill. There's also guilty by association now. Back then at the nearest pub to the train station, you knew there'd be a firm waiting for you. But if you didn't fight, you didn't get to the ground, and when you got the ground you had to fight for your life to stay there.

Back in the day, you never saw women or families going to football. It's good that that's changed.

Bill Gardner's legacy

A Legend. A total legend.

Since I've got to know him over the years, an absolute gentleman. I remember I went to his first book launch on Barking Road years ago, and we stayed at the West Ham hotel. Bonzo from Norwich was with us and there was 4-500 West Ham. All the old ICF, all the old faces. We had a right good night, right into the early hours. But I'll never forget this about Bill:

He came and knocked on my bedroom door the next morning before he left, and he said, "Thanks for coming, Boatsy, I really appreciate it. I know it was hard to come down here yesterday because there were only about two or three outsiders here." It was all pure West Ham, and he knew I'd taken quite a risk. I thought what a bloke to come down and knock on my door before he left to thank me for coming down. It felt great, and was typical of a very classy man.

19

To March or Not to March:
The Real West Ham Fans Action Group

A £20,000 Phone Call

I was phoned at home on Thursday, March 8th, 2018. It was from a gentleman claiming to represent West Ham United. It could've been a wind-up. It might not have been a wind-up. I'll let you decide after reading the following chapter. For the record, I politely told the gentleman to go fuck himself.

I didn't want his money. I couldn't sell-out what I love. I think if you sell your club out you sell anyone out, and I don't sell out to anyone. What some people don't realise is not everyone is motivated by money. Sometimes people do things for love and their life. I could never, ever take a penny off this Club, despite my belief that it's now rotten to the core.

RWHFAG

I believed I was asked to join the RWHFAG because I agreed in what they were saying. But it wasn't about that. Getting me on board was about getting bums on seats. About getting people to join the group because they trusted me, and they know I'm straight. I can get people. It don't matter what it's for, if it's over West Ham I've got a hardcore of at least 800 people who I know

I can rely on.

The people involved in the group - *some* of the people involved in the group - needed bodies. They needed a high-profile person who was maybe more articulate than them, and I went along with it. But I started to smell a rat when I wasn't invited to any of the meetings with the club. Certain people in the group told me that senior West Ham officals had called me an "unsavoury character", and "a gangster." It left a sour taste in my mouth and I was only getting piecemeal information back from the meetings that were taking place.

I'm no fool, I know when I'm being used. I was disappointed, let down and betrayed. One or two people who stayed in the group and attended the meetings were telling me what was going on, but I couldn't form a clear picture of events. After about the third meeting with the club, I learned the march had been called off. That's also when my phone started ringing off the hook.

Phone Calls and Threats

I soon became wary when I had people phoning me up telling me they'd been threatened after the march had been called off. A lot of people still wanted to march. I was invited to attend a meeting with other members of the RWHFAG where I knew I'd be asked to speak out against the march. I refused to do either.

It became clear they did not want that march to take place, which was a hell of a U-turn! I'd already started to become pissed off with the group around a month before the march was supposed to happen. There were too many meetings and not enough action. I started to back off from the group. Something didn't feel right.

Members still planning to march were being threatened. That spelled the end of the RWHFAG for me. As well as the threats, I couldn't suffer all the talk of money, badges, stickers or marches making money. It wasn't for me. I've never begrudged anyone wanting to earn a crust, but it wasn't for me. I don't want to make money out of West Ham fans. My motives have always been the best for West Ham, and anyone who knows me knows that's what I'm all about. The West Ham fans were betrayed, and I'll go to my grave believing that.

I wasn't threatened by anyone. Senior members of the group told me it was all bollocks that people were being threatened. That didn't fit in with what I was being told by people I could tell were physically shaking at the other end of the line. These were well-respected people from within the group, phoning me up saying, "Bill, I've been threatened, I wanna march but I can't." People were genuinely afraid. One told me someone had threatened to carve up his kids, another that he and his girlfriend would be 'cut up', another that his house would be burnt down.

During one conversation I did warn a gentleman I'd take the heads off anyone who came round my house. I made sure Sarah and my boys stayed home that night and sat up with my 'toolbox' next to me.

Political Infiltration

After the original march was banned, several other West Ham groups became affiliated with the RWHFAG, and the story went around they were connected to political groups. Some of them were linked to the Labour party, some to the Mayor's office, and some to various right-wing and left-wing groups. This was a West Ham fan's movement. It was never political, and I believe it was a smokescreen to discourage people from marching in future and to increase the likelihood of any future march being banned.

I think there's a lot of snowflakes at West Ham now. They melt away under the first sign of pressure instead of sticking together. The march would have had fantastic backing, no-one would've been attacked, no-one would've got hurt. I had in place the most fantastic people, some of whom had stopped going to watch West Ham after the move from Upton Park.

I was more than happy that if I went along, we would've done it. But it was too late. I'd had all the stuffing knocked out of me by that time. My love of West Ham was being eroded by greed. At the end of the day that wasn't for me. I can't stomach treachery. It's as simple as that. I felt totally let down by people I'd known for years. I'll be honest, I never ever trusted them, but I had respect for them.

You can argue the point all day long on this one. I believe West Ham is now the most corrupt club in English football, if not Europe. Everything has a price at West Ham United now. Our history's being sold off. Trophies and plaques were all auctioned off after we left our true home. But they can't buy me. There is no price. I will not sell out to anyone. Money's not that important to me. It's not like I've got a lot, but what I have got is pride in the people I've stood alongside for 45 years and I would not sell them out. But my values are not everyone's.

I didn't want their money. How do you throw away someone's life for 20 grand? What does that work out a year? Not a lot. It would have bought a new van, which I needed at the time, but how could I have looked myself in the mirror. How could I do that and say I've done the best I can for all these people, those 13,000 who joined the group?

Everything's been money orientated but what they don't realise is it's somebody's life their playing with. Somebody's passion for his or her team is very different from someone who earns money out of it. They go over there, sit in their nice warm restaurants, at half-time they have their meal, they have their food and drink on the house, they have free travel to away games, everything comes out of the club. Even the petrol they use to go to the games. But that's not the real fan. The real fan is the one who wakes up at 1 or 2 in the morning to travel away. In my case, some nights I don't even go to bed the night before an away game, so I'm on time to pick up my mates and go to football. It's never about the money. With West Ham fans it's always about the ambition to be better. To be a big club. To play on the European stage. To have your kids walk around with their heads held high, instead of being ridiculed.

A Throwback to Darker Times

The comments that were made before the march, about not walking through ICF territory, it did get to me. I was being asked to sort it out again. I did my best. I visited certain people. I received assurances. But where money's involved loyalty, honour, and dignity go out the window. Times have changed. In today's football culture money overrides everything. I thought, "I've done it once, I'm too old to do it again. Find someone else to sort it out, sort it out between ya."

When other people's fans used to come to Upton Park, they used to shit themselves. It was the worst place to come. They hated it. All fans will tell you that. Especially a night game - they didn't like it one bit. But with this new stadium it's more a case of bring your grandma, sit on the grass and have a picnic. I hate it with a vengeance.

I just want West Ham fans to know that I never sold out, that I never would sell out; I couldn't live with myself if I felt that I'd done anything to hurt West Ham, and I've always said that I would never fight another West Ham fan.

Like Winston Churchill said, 'never have so many been fucked by so few.' That's how I would describe what it's been like at West Ham over the last few years. Certain people have got to have a long look in the mirror at themselves. They don't need me to tell them. They'll feel it every morning when they look in that mirror if they've got anything about them. If they haven't, they won't think fuck all about anyone or anything but themselves.

20

Emergence of the Newbies

The times we've got there now, I'm finding it hard, very difficult. The easiest thing they could do is to ban me. I would love them to ban me because then I've got an excuse not to go.

But I can't walk away. I never want to feel that I don't love West Ham anymore. And that's what these people – Gold, Sullivan, Brady – that's what they're doing. They're making me feel like I don't love West Ham as much, and that's the thing that frightens me the most. It's like saying, "Stop loving your brother, or stop loving your sister." I don't want that to happen, but that's the way it feels right now. They're driving me, and people who feel the same as me, away because I don't believe what they're doing is good for the Club and the fans.

I don't believe the way they treat people is good. I've always been a fan, never a customer. West Ham's not a supermarket and its soul has never been up for sale to the highest bidder. Not with our history; and not until now. To be fair when I meet a lot of the people over there now, I think they're right pratts. But I look at them like you would your own kid, a naughty kid, "Oh he's a right pratt, but he's alright."

That's how I feel about a lot of them now, especially the newbies. And when I say newbies, I mean the popcorn brigade and the ones who've arrived on the scene in the last two or three years because it's cheap football for them. With the Premier League becoming a massive earner worldwide, English football has become a tourist attraction. They'll do Madame Tussauds, the London Eye, the Tate, Buck House, and then squeeze in a match. The London Stadium athletics track is as good a place as any, and you'll always get a seat. But they haven't got a clue about our roots or our culture.

They've got no history with us. They don't know what it's like to feel like a true Hammer, a true West Ham supporter. Maybe my circumstances made me a true Hammer more than most. But when I talk to people over there, very few have opened up and told me what made them a Hammer. The ones that do, nine times out of ten they'll say it was the football. But in my case, it was never the football. It was always being accepted as part of the family.

21

Leipzig

I was the little fat ginger-haired kid at primary school who got bullied all the time. I used to get called all sorts of names, Billy Bunter, Billy fork - God knows where that one come from. It was mainly because I didn't talk a lot, I was shy and had no confidence. I was a fair lump which didn't help, and I didn't dress savvy enough for the times. I was always pretty scruffy. I would have been aged between seven and nine I reckon.

These kids –including one particularly evil bastard - used to push me off the classroom chair. He'd see me there, walk over and tip it over by the legs, sending me flying. The worst part was the laughter. The whole class would crack up. It was humiliating and had a massive affect on me. No-one should be bullied, it's a cowards game. Being bullied as a kid is one of the worst things you can experience. Parents don't really know what it's like to have a bullied kid if they weren't bullied themselves. It's a horrible, horrible thing when you get home from school and you don't want to go the next day because you're frightened, or you don't want the conflict. And that's what I was like, I didn't want the conflict.

But once I had the hypnotherapy I wanted conflict all time! My confidence soared. I believe it was in me all the time, the therapy just brought it out. I'm not angry person. I get angry, but I'm not an angry person. I like to think the people who've been in my company think I can have a laugh, that I can come out with a few one liners. But I am what I am, and when I do lose my rag I've noticed people who've not seen that side of me thinking, "Fucking hell, is he the same bloke? He's a fucking lunatic." I can see it in their eyes. I can tell what they're thinking. I don't like feeling like that. I don't like people who are mates thinking, "Oh he's alright, it's not true what they say about him." Then they see me lose it and they see me in a different light. It's happened a few times and I don't like that feeling like that at all.

I fucking hated school. I never wanted to go. I met a kid who bullied me at school again when I was 18. He didn't recognise me. I said, "alright mate," and he looked at me.

I said, "do you remember me? He said, "no, sorry mate".

"I went to school with you," I told him. The poor sod didn't have a clue what was happening before he remembered me. "Oh, Bill Gardner," he said, it as if we was back at school.

"How's it going Billy B....?"

I smashed him before he could finish his sentence. He was on the floor. I only hit him once but his teeth had gone through his lip. I said, "You fucking remember now don't you." He lay there motionless and moaning. I thought, "shall I give him an hiding", and then thought "nah, he's had enough." That was a huge yoke off me. I felt like I'd got back a little of my self-respect from those school years when I had no confidence at all.

Mental Health

Everyone close to me has had their say on what they think I've got. Is it depression? Bi-Polar? Split-personality? It depends on what sort of day I'm having. Some days I'll feel great and take the Mrs out to the pictures or go for a nice walk by the lakes not too far from where we live. At other getting through the day is fucking hard work. I won't move and won't want to talk to anyone. I get really big highs and really low lows. A Jekyll and Hyde sort of character. As long as I can keep the 'bad bastard' at bay I'm alright. I'm a very emotional man, I get upset about anything and everything. I don't like to see people suffering, I don't like cruelty to animals. I don't like old people getting hit for their money. Whenever it's happened in front of me, if someone's being silly or being horrible, I can never turn the other cheek. It's not in my nature. I have to sort it out, so I do.

The depression has probably been there for years. My childhood experiences didn't help, but both my mum and my dad had it, so it may well run in the family. It brings on those feelings of utter loneliness, utter despair that I had when I was living on the streets. Homeless people in London usually mix in little groups, whether it's for protection, or having someone to talk to. They're not all blaggers, they're not all ponces. A lot of them are ill, mentally ill. A lot of them have been abused. A lot of them have fallen on hard times or they've lost somebody and they've gone to pieces, and it's a bad thing. All of us are vulnerable, and we're all only at a very small thread away from being in the same boat.

There's no point denying there's ain't an angry side to me. He rears his head in those situations where a raging fury takes over me. It smothers me, consumes me. When it's taken over there's nothing I can do to control it.

It comes up from your stomach and it goes to your brain, and you think he's taking the piss out of me. I used to think destroy him, destroy him. So I would. And then the other side of me would think what the fuck have you done? What have you done? It might sound crazy, but taming 'angry Bill' became a struggle when the new owners arrived with their empty promises and contempt for the fans. Now, in older life, I've mellowed, and see things differently. I don't see that part of me that often anymore. It's more rare because I don't get myself into situations where it has to happen.

That's not the person I am, the real me. The other one ain't the one who loves animals, walks old ladies across the road. He's totally fucking different to that. He's a horrible cunt and I hate him. He don't come out much now, not as much as he used to at any rate. He used to be out quite a lot, and once I used to get them raging fury's there was no stopping me. I was incensed, I was beyond control. Anyone trying to calm me down had no chance. Once I went I went. Given my childhood experiences, I think he developed a mind of his own to protect me.

To be fair I'm saying this now and I sound like a right lunatic. I used to totally lose the plot. And I used to find that strength I never thought I had. Once it was done I'd go back to being how I am 95 per cent of the time. Normal, respectful, trying to live a good life. But once them rages took me over, it wasn't nice. I didn't want to do that, and like I say I used to think why have I done this. One of my regrets is that on occasions, certainly with West Ham, I went too far.

It's hard to predict how I'm going to feel from one dy to the next, which in itself is fucking frustrating. It last's for days, and only takes little things. I don't like seeing people upset. I hate seeing little children who are hurt, that gets me going. I hate hearing how people have been abused and ain't got nothing. I suppose it sparks those dark old memories I still have as a kid. I think that maybe sparks me off. But I just get on with it. I walk a lot now and I love nature. I just get on with my life the best I can.

The last time 'angry Bill' came out of any note was was in Leipzig for a West Ham pre-season friendly; I was 57 at the time.

We played Dynamo Dresden, a team called Erith or something, and Cottbus. We were on the Polish borders, but we stayed in Leipzig. There was about 40 or 50 of us having a drink in a bar. We'd been out and had a nice meal, six or eight of us had a nice drop of wine when two lads came up the road. One of them had a bandage on his head with blood on it. I thought they were West Ham fans and asked, "What's happened?" One of them said, "We just got done by the Germans, but they had strange accents. "Where do you come from?" I asked. They said they were Croatians. I asked if they were West Ham fans and they replied no.

I said, "Come and have a drink with us." I got them over. I was with my mate John Waddell, a few other lads. Enough witnesses to see it any rate. I bought them a drink but didn't really have a conversation with them. They got pissed over the course of a while, and started acting up. They started saying things like, "your country's fucked, we shag your women." I looked at my mate John and he looked at me as if to say fuck 'em off out of it before there's trouble. I said, "Lads you gotta fuck off because you're getting outrageous." I carried on talking to my mates, looked round, and they're still there. I said, "Look, just fuck off!" and they've both jumped up and they've gone "you fuck off." So I walked over to them and let them have it. I've smashed them both, no more than two or three punches. I think someone's hit one of them the head with a flower pot on the way down. He looked like one of the characters out of Bill and Ben, the flower men with massive flower pot was on his head. It was hilarious. They were about 28 or 29 these fellas, but I done them both easy. These were the geezer's who hours earlier I'd helped!

So they got up and fucked off. I got out the way before the Old Bill turned up. I went through the backstreets with a couple of other lads trying to get back to the hotel. Meanwhile the police had these Croatians in a van. A van picked me up, took me back, and the two lads ID'd me through the fucking window of the van. To make matters worse the doorman in the nightclub grassed me up because I'd had a little altercation with him earlier, because they wouldn't let us into the nightclub. There was no reason for them not to. I just told them we were going in the nightclub later whether they liked it or not. I said, "You can have it easy or hard. Whichever way you want. We're no problem." Once I'd been ID'd they took me up to the police station. I had a white shirt on and I noticed that I had a red stain down it. It could've been blood. It could've been red wine. I wasn't sure so I was hiding it. I put my hand over it as they started asking me questions. I said, "look mate, before we start can I go toilet?" He said, "yeah, go on". In the toilet, I've got hold of my shirt, put water on it and rubbed it for England. Luckily it came off. "I'm in the clear on that one," I said to myself.

When I came out the desk sergeant looked up and said, "What's the dark patch on your shirt?"

"Can this night get any fuckin' worse?" I thought.
"I've just had a wash mate," I replied. "I'm 57 years old, and I'm tired. It's four o'clock in the morning." My mates were outside the station trying to get me out. Some of them went beyond the call of duty, they really did. One of them ran about three miles to

find the police station. What they did was marvelous, "and I'd like to thank them again for trying to help me.

The Senior Officer said, "You attacked these two lads." I said, "Look mate, I'm nearly 60-years-old, I'm in ill health, them lads had already been in one fight before we helped them. I haven't been spoken to by anybody, do you think they're going to believe this in court, that this old man can beat up these two big fellas in their 20's? Will that get you a result?" He told me they were gong to watch the CCTV and that while enquiries were pending they'd let me out on bail. I said, "are you going to give me a lift back to the hotel then?" The copper said, "yeah, give him a lift." So the same ones who'd nicked me took me back. I'm feeling a bit cocky now. They'd already spun the hotel room room to see if they could find anything incriminating and come up with nothing.

While waiting for my lift back to the hotel they contacted London, told them about me, and what had happened. Meanwhile I said to the other coppers, "Let's have a game. Am I innocent or guilty? Three of them said innocent. The sergeant said guilty. I said to him, "that's why you're the sergeant" and laughed. They said they were going through the CCTV footage, which they never even had. There was no CCTV evidence, but I didn't know that at the time. On the way home I was expecting them to pull me at the airport and throw me in the nick. They were nowhere to be seen. As I got on the plane all the boys started whistling the song from 'the great escape' which did make me chuckle. I did throw a wobbler that night. I felt betrayed. I would've done more damage, without a doubt. I hadn't been like that for a long while. It was like going out on the beer and I got the taste. It'd been a long while. These boys took the piss out of me. They'd had my beer. They'd had my company. They'd had my friendship. They abused it, so I abused them.

When I showed kindness to these two and they threw shit in my face, it's more than you can bear. I tried to be fair with them. I tried to be alright. Unfortunately it didn't work.

If my mate John hadn't moved heaven and earth and pulled me off them I would've probably killed them. Stone dead. John said that to me. By then I'd lost it and I didn't have a clue what was going on. That part of me don't come out of too much now thankfully.

I believe my early life and the situations I was in manifested themselves in later life through violence. As I've explained, sometimes it was excessive, sometimes not enough. It's just the way it happened. Years of anger, frustration, and abuse. Different people have different coping mechanisms. Mine was violence. When my mum and dad were rowing a home I used to hide under the table. I've seen my mum do some daft things. They'd have a row and she'd pick something up and hit my dad round the head with it. I've seen my mum give my dad some proper, proper whacks. But never once did I see him lay his hands on her. She used to tell people he did, but he never did. She used to put lipstick and make up on her neck and make out he'd strangled her. I was with her when she told a friend. "This is what he done to me, my neck, my poor neck." But I used to see her putting that that make up on. I would've been about nine or ten. But my dad never ever laid his hands on my mum. My old man was gentleman. His own upbringing - which I didn't know too much about till he died - might not have been the best in the world, but he was alright.

But at the end of the day my mum was the violent one, she'd fight anything with two legs. If weren't unheard of for her to leap over the shop counter and give the shop-owner a proper dig.

Lonely in a crowd

You can be in a large group of people, you can be in great company, you can be in amongst mates. But you can still feel lonely inside. It's something I've always believed because I've felt it loads of times. You can be lonely in a crowd. There's a lot of people that'll carry on like they're the life and soul of the party. But deep inside they're hurt and they're cut up about something. But they won't be honest with themselves. They're consumed by what other people will think of them. I ain't bothered what other people think. I tell the truth how it is for me. If by my being open about it people can say, "you know what, I feel a bit like that," then I've done what I wanted to do.

When I was on my own in that graveyard night after night, with very little sleep, I'd just sit there and think. I'd analyse things, try and read a bit, then analyse myself a bit more. Back then every day was a bonus, even if it didn't feel like one. In moments of weakness I'd start to wonder, would it be nice to not wake up tomorrow? To end it. To just go.

To just fuck everyone off and go, and let everyone get on with it.

'Angry Bill' wouldn't have it, but, without doubt, West Ham, and my West Ham family, saved me from myself in those early years without even knowing it.

22

Neil, Scobie, Lol

Brothers and life-long Hammer's supporters Colin (Scobie) and Lawrence (Lol) Schofield's friendship with Bill stretches back to the late 60's, fermented in the cauldron of Upton Park's Chicken Run, as well as those decrepit old trains to away games.

Neil Duggan first met Bill on the Bramall Lane terraces in 1977, as serious trouble flared inside and outside the stadium between rival supporters.

"I took a clump and Bill had a bloodied nose," he recalls. "He sort of took me under his wing that day."

Since those early days - doing whatever they had to do get to away games - children, wives and girlfriends have changed the landscape. The four however remain good mates and a tight unit.

Their respective children are mates and are all, needless to say, staunch West Ham United supporters, been to games together, on some occasions with dads in tow. A 'West Ham family', you might say.

Prior to meeting Bill tells me: "I trust them three blokes completely. True friends. I don't say that lightly, cos in general I don't trust anybody. I rely on myself, I back myself, and I trust myself. But this lot, I'd trust them with my family."

That was put severely to the test following Bill's ban from Upton Park, the place he defined more than any other as home, in 1988.

Neil: That broke his heart, the ban. It really hit him hard. You've got to remember he'd not long lost his old man and Bill don't miss West Ham games. It just don't happen. He loves the Club. That ban really cut him up.

Lol: We used to take James (Bill's son) to the football when Bill was banned. It's fair to say he weren't in a good way.

He'd turn up opposite the main gates with James on a match day, and he'd go, "here, watch this". He'd walk in one direction and the old bill cameras started following him.

He'd walk back towards us and they followed him back. We'd cross the road to get in and he'd come with us to say bye to James, to give him a kiss, and all these Old Bill were just stood there, watching him.

It was hard for him, fucking hard. I personally think the Old Bill were gutted he hadn't tried getting in because they couldn't nick him.

First encounters

Lol: We first saw Bill at Whitechapel Station in the late 60's. I spotted this big lad walking along the platform, all permed, curly hair and that.

I saw him walking over to Ted. They was chatting so I thought he must be alright, what with Ted being one half of the TBF.

He was a bit shy, but he did chat to everyone. It was just football, West Ham, nothing personal or anything like that. I reckon he was about 15, 16 but he was a fuckin unit even then. He just fitted in. He weren't flash, looked like he could handle himself and didn't mind a laugh at his own expense.

Scobie: After that we used to see him at all the away games. Straight away I realised he was a bit of a lad. I don't know about shy, but he was a very private person. He still is unless you know him very, very well. But he was like that as a nipper to be honest.

Neil: He's always ploughed his own furrow. Like that night at Sheffield United. We came unstuck in their end and got led across the pitch.

That was the first time I got to know him cos he kind of took me under his wing a little bit that day and there was only a few of us there. No-one would've told him to do that. He just does what he thinks is right. Fuck the rest.

Lol: What made me laugh was in Carlton's film was where they portrayed Bill as this fucking fat bloke with dark hair and a dark tasche. I thought, "fuck me they've done him up like a fuckin Scouser!

Neil: That bloke looked more like Jim McDonnell out of Corry that Bill!

Lol: In fairness he was always up for a laugh Bill. But he had to get to know you, know what I mean? As far as we were concerned all we was doing was meeting up at fuckin Kings Cross or Mile End about eight in the morning, going to the game and getting home about 10 or 11 at night.

Yeah there might have been a few fun and games but the way we saw it, we was just having a laugh. People looked at that as hooliganism. But we were just having a laugh all the way there and all the way back.

A Suit and a Tall story

Smokies Nightclub
Oldham, 2001

Lol: We was on our way to Blackburn that day we lost 7-1. We thought we'd make a weekend of it and ended up in Smokies.

We'd been taking the piss out of Bill cos he had this suit on, fuck me, it was a white double wide dog-tooth suit, he really thought he was he business, John Travolta and that.

He waltzed over to us giving it large, thinking he was the proper bollocks, but to be fair the club lights weren't too flattering on this suit he was wearing.

He come up and goes, "what do you reckon?" I looked him up and down and said, "Bill, you look like a negative of Idi Amin." He didn't see the funny side but the rest of us did. He stormed off to the bar I think.

They knew we were West Ham and up there for the game, that lot in the club, but they were alright and this geezer starts palling me up, chatting to me, telling me all these things he's done and whatever.

Then he goes "you've got that Bill Gardner ain't ya. My brother put through him through the Wimpy bar window in Manchester."

I said "Really?"

"Yeah, yeah, he goes," and calls his brother over. The bloke's brother tells him what we've been talking about and he looks at us. "You lads know Bill Gardner?

"Yeah, we've seen him about."

"Game fucker," he goes. "Proper geezer."

"Oh so you know him then?" I asked.

"Yeah. We had it off and I sent him through the Wimpy bar window in Manchester. I've got a lot of respect for him like, top fucking geezer."

"Oh right. You sure it was Bill Gardner?" He says yeah. I said "hold on a minute mate". I've turned round, caught Bill's attention and nodded for him to come over.

Bill comes over, looks at the fella who clearly don't know him from Adam, then looks at me.

"What?" he says, still pissed off about the suit remark.

"Bill, this is the man who reckons he put you through the window of the Wimpy bar in Manchester."

I've turned to the bloke and just said, "Alright mate, this is my friend Bill Gardner."

The look on the bloke's face was priceless. He went whiter than Bill's suit!

Bill smiled, shook his hand, and you could just see the agony in the bloke's face. You could almost hear his fucking knuckles cracking as Bill squeezed his hand harder and harder.

To be fair to Bill he just turned round and laughed at him. He leaned in the bloke's ear and said, "I wish I had a fucking fiver for everyone who reckons they've done me. Not a mark on my body, not a mark on my face, never been nicked."

We didn't see much of that fella after that.

European nights

Neil: We went to Bucharest in the Uefa Cup. It was just after the Ceausescu regime so it was a bit manic. A load of our party got robbed or mugged. Our hotel owners controlled these brasses who'd go in there at night for the West Ham fans.

The hotel bar was full of them and the bloke on the door was taking money off them to let them sit and drink in there, you know, tap up the clientele and that.

One of them has taken a right shine to Bill, a real right shine. She says to him, "you remind me of my favourite TV star, Telly Savalas"

"Well course we all pissed ourselves. I mean fucking Kojak was a new one on me! I don't know who it was, but someone's shouted, "who's she remind you of Bill?"

"Pat fucking Butcher on a bad day," he replied.

Everyone was in bits, except this big Romanian woman who didn't have a clue what was so funny.

Lol: That's the thing about Bill. People don't think he can have a laugh, or laugh at himself even. But he can. He's just got to know ya and trust ya.

Neil: Yeah. You have to know him really well to get away with it. He doesn't suffer fools lightly and if he don't know you and thinks you're taking the piss you'll know about it.

Close to The Madding Crowd

The West Ham United fanbase is renowned for its passion, loyalty and devotion to the Club. As such, Bill's standing within the extended group, forged over three decades, is one which continues to attract well-wishers, hand-shakers, the grateful, storytellers, and the nostalgic. As Bill says he is humbled by the affection that goes with the territory of being Mr West Ham.

Scobie, Lol and Neil have their own views.

Neil: With Bill, these two [Scobie, and Lol] will tell you, he's always got time to talk to any West Ham fan. I mean, us three are not quite so tolerant. There's been many a time I've asked him, "what you doing talking to that melt?" or something like that. But Bill, because he's good hearted, he'll talk to any West Ham fan.

Lol: I've been with him and people just want to come up and talk to him and he's giving them the time of day, saying hello, how are you mate and all that.

He tries to move away they fucking come round as if they're attached to him, and they carry on talking to him. And I see him look as if to say, "I wish they'd fuck off", but he never, ever says it.

He just tolerates them. He said to me last night (TBF reunion, The Vic, Plaistow) if one more person fucking kisses me I'm gonna knock 'em out. He was joking, but I think there was a bit of truth to it.

Scobie: I've told him, I've said what do you keep talking to people for. "Ahh they're West Ham," he says. Even at West Ham I've seen people who don't know him carrying on like they're his best mate.

Lol: I've stood outside that Erkans, that fish and chip shop by the old Chicken Run. Me and Neil used to go and have a fucking kebab or something. I'd say come on let's go cos Bill's holding court in the middle of the shop. We'd just back away.

Neil: It was surreal. Someone would come along, shake Bill's hand, talk to him for about five minutes, he'd go, and when you look there's a load of people cueing up.

Scobie: Yeah, they was cuing up to shake Bill's hand and have a chat with him. It used to drive me fucking mad.

Neil: Oh mate he's got time for everyone

Lol: I don't think it's cos he wants to be wanted. It's not that at all. It's respect. Whereas the likes of us would turn round and say "do us a favour mate, fuck off," Bill would never, ever do that to a West Ham fan.

Scobie. 100 per-cent.

Neil: He'd help anyone out, right. So it's one them audiences with him to go and say, "oh hello Bill, I don't know if you remember me, but you told me if I'd had any problems you'd come and help me out. Well I've got this problem," and Bill would be like, "yeah ok mate, no problem."

Lol: When he turned up last night and all those people were rushing over to say hello, I thought I'll give him a bit of time. When I went over there I could just tell by the look on his face he was just saying to me, "Get me out of here mate." He doesn't like adulation. He never has. I think sometimes he don't mind it, but it can get too much.

Scobie: But he's brought a lot of that on himself. For doing what we've said. And I've told him, cos I could say anything to Bill. He might be upset for five minutes, but then all of a sudden he'll fuckin snap out of it and that'll be it. It'll be done. It's concern for a mate.

Lol: Let's just say, all of those people at the pub last night. How many of them can say they stood side by side with the man?

Lol, Scobie, Bill…and a packet of dried Chilies

Lol: Every time we went to football whatever you had, whatever snack you had, Bill wanted some. Fuck me he could eat for England. So whatever you had he wanted some.

So me and him (Scobie) went out on a Friday night for a pizza, a Pizza Express. And they always have on the table a little fucking bowl or jar of chilies, dried chilies on the table.

Fuck it I thought, I emptied them into my pocket. He (Scobie) says, "Yeah have the cunt". I think he knew what I was up to.

Scobie: It didn't take a lot of working out!

Lol: At the next home game I brought one of those bags of mixed nuts and raisins, opened it up, put the fuckin chilies in and shook it up. Bill turns up and straight away he's at it. "What you got there? What you got there boys?"

"Nuts and raisins Bill," I said.

"Give us some" he says. Course, he's got hands like fucking shovels ain't he. So I've poured a load in and he went "lovely".

We're watching the game but I've got an eye on Bill, throwing millions of these fucking nuts and raisins down his gullet. Then he stopped chewing and his head started going bright red. He turned to look at me.

I think he was about to say something before BANG! Fuck me, he's only exploded everywhere, gobbing out all these fuckin nuts and raisins and chili's! He just spat it all out!

This fucking poor bloke in front of him, it all went in his fucking jacket hood. This is in the fucking Chicken Run, you know what I mean!? Everyone's thinking, "Shit, who's wound Bill up!"

He was livid. "You cunts!" he was shouting, 'you fucking cunts! But it was so funny cos his head could've stopped traffic.

Scobie: He got hold of us both and fucking whacked our heads together. The next game I had these sweets. "Want one of these Bill?" I asked.

"No I fucking don't!" he says.

The Talented Mr Scratcher

Neil: Of course he's the one (Lol) responsible for the wind-up in Bill's first book, the one where he had that group photo and Bill's asked Lol, "who's that bloke at the end? I mean, fancy asking him!

Lol: I think we were down at the Manor Rugby Club. We had a picture done of all of us, and this fucking lad Murphy got in on the end.

So we said, "Oi! This is for us, you know, our little firm." But he wouldn't fuck off. So when Bill emailed me asking for the names of everyone in the photo, I thought I'm fucked if Murphy's having his name in there.

I gave him all the proper names but when it come to Murphy I gave him the name "Dick Scratcher". The book comes out, and fuck me, there he is, Murphy, large as life on the fuckin page having the time of his life.

I read the names underneath and sure enough the very last name reads "Dick Scratcher". I fuckin pissed myself!

Neil: Read it in the book, it's in there! The nearest I've come to winding Bill up was when he got banged up at Leipzig or Dresden, one of them places. He got arrested and banged up.

A few weeks later we're back home and Bill gets a letter from from the German authorities.

He was proper worried the letter was a summons and he'd have to go back to Germany to stand trial. He gets on the blower to me. "Neil, I've got this letter, it's all in German, I think I got to go back mate."

I got my Mrs. to translate the letter as she does all that at work. It said: "Dear Mr. Gardner, you were here on this date for this matter, no charges have been brought, that's the end of the matter."

Now the question I've got to ask myself is do I have some fun with this or not? I've gotta admit, it took every ounce of willpower to not ring him up and say: "Yeah you gotta go back mate. Good news is you can do the time over here if you get found guilty. That's a result ennit?"

But I couldn't do it. Not after everything he'd been through.

Lol/Scobie: (Simultaneously) I would of!

Lol: What a lot of people can't get is, if the piss was there to be taken, there was none of this, "oh don't do it to him or him, if the piss was there to be taken the piss got taken.

Neil: That went for Bill as much as anyone else, but he wouldn't have had it any other way.

Lol: And he was an east target because he's so fucking trusting! Don't get me wrong; Bill knows the ways of the world more than most.
  But when it comes to a wind-up and things like that, fuck me…how can I say it. Winding Bill up is the easiest thing in the world. I just wouldn't recommend doing it if he don't know you!

Scobie: He believes people and he believes in people don't he. He's a trusting person. That's his nature.

Bill the Man

Neil: The one thing I'd say about Bill is that he was never a bully. One or two people who hung around with us were, but that could never be said of Bill.

Lol: No, never. I've seen him dig West Ham supporters out for being bullies at games, you know, you'll see the ones who all get fucking pissed up like they get, digging out other teams fans.
  I mean, they might be slagging off a fucking father and son or father and daughter or whatever. That's not how West Ham fans operate.
  Bill will just straighten the West Ham out, you know, "Oi! They're supporting their fucking team. Sort your fucking selves out." And they do.

Neil: On the flight back from Osijek a few years ago there was this right arsehole. He was proper pissed, giving the stewardesses a right hard time, know what I mean? Proper pissed, proper lairy.

Anyway Bill's had enough of this so he's got up, marched down the paisle towards the geezer and gone, "Oi! Treat her with some fucking respect'. It started raring up a bit, you know.

But the funniest thing was once Bill started down the plane all you could hear was the 'click click, click' of a load of fucking seatbelts being undone. Everyone was thinking, "If Bill's gonna have a tear up we're in" sort of thing.

Lol: Another thing, he's got two boys and they're not involved in any trouble at all.

Neil: Nicest lads you'd ever wish to meet. We've watched them grow up from little kids, and they've been the nicest kids.

Lol: They've never wanted anything to do with that side of football. And I'm not criticising other people, but it weren't for them and that's all about the way they were raised.

James and Dan know his background and his history, so I think it's a compliment to him and Sarah.

Crossed wires at Tottenham

Lol: A few seasons back, some of the boys went to Tottenham away. Me and Scobie was on holiday, so my boy Brad and his mate had our tickets.

I said go and meet Bill and Danny at Barking, so you'll be with a little crowd then and you'll be safe. Ted had organised the meet the way he always does for Spurs away, and some of his lot were there so I knew he'd be double safe.

So they take the push and pull train from Barking to South Tottenham and go into this pub. After a bit Bill says he didn't wanna drink anymore, so about 10 of them start walking up Tottenham High Road towards the ground, which is a fuckin' trek and a half.

And there are all these little fucking spotters all the way up, all the little Tottenham spotters. As they got a bit further up they said a mob of about 40-50 come along, and one of them right at the front went, "Oi! Gardner, I've been fucking after you for years." Bill just laughed at him and goes, "Yeah, I probably done your old man as well."

But they was right on it. "You've lost it Gardner, come on then, let's have it," and all that bollocks.

Bill thought fuck this.

He pushed Danny into this shop doorway, took off his hat, put it in his pocket, walked into the middle of the road and said "come on then you mug, you got the bottle?"

Neil: This is only about 4-5 seasons ago. He was all about protecting the kids that day.

Lol: My Brad stood next to him. He stood next to him with Ted, Moose, and Brad said one other bloke who he didn't know.

But the five of them just stood there, and this Tottenham supporter come along and said "Come on then Gardner, " but he didn't really do much else. The geeza had all the mouth but he wouldn't meet Bill in the road.

Scobie: No-one's ever had the bottle.

Lol: I thought it was a bit embarrassing when I heard about it to be honest. You either do something or you don't. It's as simple as that. If you don't fancy it, then fuck off and let us get to the game. If you do here we are on your manor, your fucking move.

This other Tottenham fella said, "Oh c'mon look, he's with his fuckin kid." He said "there's nothing brave or honorable doing a bloke with his kid there," which was a respectable thing to say.

But all these others were just giving it all the mouth, and Bill, Ted and and the rest of them were just stood there in the middle of the road saying "well fucking do something then!" A couple of coppers turned up on horses and started calling the Tottenham firm out by name, like, "come on Bob," or "come on John, get back," and all that.

And it stops. It's over.

Me and Scobie got back from holiday the next day so we didn't know anything about it. The following day I get a call from our mate Paul who lives up in Coventry and knows one of the Chelsea boys. He says to me, "what's all this about Gardner bottling it against Tottenham?

I said, "What you on about?"

"I heard Tottenham come for him and Bill had to call the old bill to protect him," he says.

I said, "Give me 10 minutes. I'll call you back." I phoned my Brad, who like I say was there and told him what Paul had said.

Straight away he says, "What a load of bollocks!" He said when Bill walked out into Tottenham High Road not one of them took a step forward. He said there was a good 40 or 50 of them, but not of them stepped forward.

I asked Brad what he would've done you have if it had kicked off. "Probably ended up on the slab next to at least one of them," he said.

They love giving it to Bill, he's the one they still want even though he's in his 60's. Not that it's ever bothered him.

Scobie: That's cos no-one's ever done him and everyone wants to be the first.

Neil: He gets recognised everywhere. If we was to go up to Tottenham now he'd get recognised straight away, straight away. I guarantee you.

Lol: He gets recognised everywhere, everywhere West Ham go.

The Erdington Monster

Lol: We went to the semi-final at Villa Park in 1980 where we played Everton. We stayed at a Hotel in Erdington. Bill brought the girl he was seeing at the time, Jan I think it was.

Scobie: Yeah, it was Jan.

Lol: So we've all driven up to the game, and we stayed in this hotel in Erdington. It was a big old house really. Bill had a room on the ground floor with bay windows and he was in there with Jan. So anyway we've all gone out on the piss.

Now clearly some of us don't know when we've had enough, and a few of us went off to a nightclub. Bill's gone back early, well early. So we try this nightclub – I think it was called the

Rumrunner, it was supposed to be the top nightclub in Birmingham or something. But they wouldn't let us in.

So my mate Gary's gone, "do you know who I am?" The bloke's gone, "no, who are ya?" "I'm Simon Le Bon's brother" says Gary, and in we went! So anyway, I've had my fill and said I want to go. I left a few West Ham in there; fuck knows how they felt at the game the next day.

I've asked the driver for the Erdington Hotel or the Sunbury Hotel in Erdington, something like that, then I said I wanted the Burberry Hotel in Sunbury Road, totally fucked it up, and fuck me the driver got me there! I can't explain how he did, he just did!

I was in the back of this cab and all I can see is motorway lights and signs. I'm thinking this is gonna cost me an arm and a leg. We stopped and the bloke's gone "fiver alright mate?" "Sorted", I thought…until I realise I've got no fucking door key.

It's now fucking 3am. So very gently I tap on the window to Bill's room. "Bill, Bill", I was whispering probably loud as fuck. I couldn't bang too loud cos it would've woke the whole house up or I'd have ended up putting the window through.

A bit louder. "Bill, Bill, Bill…" All of a sudden I see a little movement in the curtains. I'm thinking thank fuck. "Bill, Bill, let me in mate, I ain't got me key."

Then fucking ET poked his head through the window and I nearly shat myself. It was Bill and he'd fucking stuck his knob through the curtains! I went "let me in please Bill, you're me best mate and all that."

So he comes to the door, and fuck me he opens it stark bollock naked, sporting a massive fucking hard-on!

I rather stupidly said, "what you up to?

"What do you fucking think I'm up!" he tries to whisper back at me. I was pissing myself laughing. He fucking got off the job to answer the door!

Neil: Like I said, Bill would do anything to help out a mate!

23

Man United with the Mile End Mob

By the early '70s my name was getting mentioned more and more. I didn't go looking for it, it just did. I wouldn't have said I was part of the Mile End Mob at that time. I was just one of their mates. Eventually, once I'd earned their respect, I was a sort of honorary member if you like. It's not like there's an application form or anything! But it was an honour because I was the only one not from the manor, from Mile End. They all knew each other, they all lived on the estates around Mile End in the flats. I had to earn their respect to become part of that group. They were all bad boys but good boys, if you know what I mean. There's no doubt about that. I just showed them that I would back them and never back down.

It used to go off every other week. It went off and you stood. It'd be like having a fry-up in the morning. You had your breakfast, went to the game, a row was there to be had and you stood.

No one game stands out, but there's been quite a few. We did go into the Shed together at Chelsea one year. We came in late on the left-hand side of the Shed, through the gate. They used to have this little chant: "Miiiiile End, Miiiiile End," and fuck me, it used to put the fear of God into people! I got told that by other teams' supporters. They knew they weren't fucking around, that these boys could really have it.

West Ham took the Shed that day. Mile End turned up, and they ran. Simple as that. They didn't want to know.

I wouldn't say I was excited or anything. By then it had become like going to work for me. The excitement had died a long time before that. It was a job done, forget it, move on. But at the time it was something you had to do.

I first met the Mile End the day we went to Old Trafford. It was early, around 1970-71. It might even have been 1969. About 30-40 of us went right in the middle of the Stretford End. As always we waited until the teams came out because it took the coppers longer to get to you and they weren't expecting it. Once the teams were out, we started singing *Bubbles* and it'd go off all around us. It was ferocious fighting at Man United that day. The Old Bill came in and moved us to the top of the Stretford End, in the corner. Nowadays they'd take you out, but they put us right in the corner with a line of coppers around us. They (Manchester United) steamed into us so many times it was unbelievable. I lost count of the number of times they attacked us. They'd come through the coppers' lines so we stood there and had it with them. One of our lads got carried out on a stretcher. I remember seeing it was Jeffrey, the programme seller at Upton Park, in his usual leather coat. God knows why he came in with us, he got carried out on a stretcher after two minutes! As they were taking him around the pitch, I remember thinking, "What the fuck's he doing in here?" and then we got in the corner.

Cage Fighting and Banana Bob

On the way home there were loads of Manchester United supporters on the train, and the trains used to have big areas for mail on one of the carriages. You could probably get around 60-70 pushbikes in there. But apart from some newspapers and magazines, they'd be empty. We called it the cage. A lot of the trains were so full up we stood in the cage. So, we put a few Man United in there for a bit of sport. We used to get the mouthy ones from London, go up to them, and say, "Come on then, in the cage." They'd go in, one against one in the cage, nobody butted in, and then it was, "Next!" or, "go get another one, this one's had enough." It was like lions picking off antelopes. It was very gladiatorial. I did it once, Joey Williams did it once, and another lad did it once that day.

They were fucking horrible back then, Manchester United. I know some of them now, and they aren't too bad but I'll be honest with you, in them days they were real proper flash, and there weren't as many from London like there is now. They had this fella called Sammy the Engine. I think they called him that because he always steamed in. He was quite a tasty old boy; he could have a row.

Then there was Banana Bob. The famous Banana Bob, a huge bloke and notorious Cockney red. The worst of the worst for me. I was sitting on the train; he didn't know who I was. I was coming home from Manchester after we played Man United and just talking to people. We had this bloke behind us in my earhole, and all I could hear was him mouthing off. "Yeah we went to Orient last week, I turned a pram over." 1974 that would be, because I'd just had my little girl.

I got up and I said to him, "You've got a fucking big mouth you have."

"What you on about?" he said.

"Come on, I'll fight ya."

He kept asking, "What d'ya mean?"

I said, "Well you're such a hard man turning over prams, go on I'll fight you now."

I used to wear a big belt in them days with studs in it. I took the belt off and threw it on the table.

"Here you go," I said to him. "You can have that."

He just looked at me, so I told him, "Get out of that fucking chair or I'll do ya where you sit."

He got up and I just went bang, bang, bang. Three punches and that was it, all over. Some hard man!

Someone took a tenner off him but I said to whoever it was to give it back to him. Afterall, we weren't fucking muggers.

24

Stuart Slater

Former West Ham striker Stuart Slater retuned to the club at the age of 31, where, unbeknown to him, he would go on to coach Bill's son, Dan. It led to an encounter between coach and parent which Stuart still vividly recalls some 20 years later. Before recounting this little-known tale, the player once described by Bobby Moore as "the future of English football", and whom the late Sir Bobby Robson earmarked for future stardom, briefly recounts his footballing journey from leafy country village-life, to the altogether less sedate surroundings of east London.

Obviously the east end people they can be quite chirpy, they can be quite opinionated. But they are incredibly passionate people. They love their football and they love their club. West Ham United is literally all that matters for many, many people in east London, stretching all the way out into deepest Essex. Whereas Ipswich and other club's fans, no disrespect, can be quite reserved, West Ham fans that are an incredibly passionate, honest, and loyal. They'll back you 100 per-cent as long as you put a shift in and don't take liberties with them or the Club. As a player wearing that famous shirt you knew you had to put a shift in. There was also a certain way of playing which, when Ron (Greenwood) spoke about the West Ham way, meant playing with a bit of style. Sometimes that doesn't win games, but they love to be entertained, and it's up to the players to get them on the edge of their seats. They're a knowledgeable bunch about one and two-touch football for example. It's like a religion for them. It's their club. They want you to do well, or they want you to play well, or they want to have some entertainment.

They look forward to watching their club. They work their socks off all week, they're working class people and they work they're socks off. They know what it's like to earn some money. When they pay good money to watch you, they expect a shift in return. If you show that, and they got some entertainment, the place is rocking. And that's what makes an amazing atmosphere, you know, especially under lights. They've worked hard all day, and they've looked forward to the game and then they see somebody like Dicksy or Bonzo making a challenge and then they see some flair like Alan Devonshire and Trevor Brooking, and they love it. They show their emotions, their passion, and their love for the club. It's a unique experience for a player from Suffolk!

On the terraces

Growing up, from where I was from in Suffolk, I as so oblivious to any sort of hooliganism. You saw it a little bit on the TV in the 80's.

Once I arrived at West Ham as a schoolboy, I gradually started to become more aware of it as a player. You were aware West Ham fans had a bit of a reputation. They're hard working people and tough cookies and love their club.to bits. And yeah, I did see the odd incident from time to time.

Did the players ever talk about it?

I was aware of it when I was an apprentice, so when I got into the first team, sort of 17, 18, really my closest colleagues were probably Georgie Parris, Pottsy, Dicko, Kevin Keen. We didn't really talk about it. But in my apprentice group, we had some people that lived in the area, people like Simon Livett who lived in East Ham. We'd go training in the morning and we'd go to his mum and dads in the afternoon, and walk to the ground for the game.

That's how close his family lived, and he was very aware of it. By that time I'd get on the tube and sometimes spot the "ICF Congratulations, cards.

So you were aware of it and you could see the intensity of the fanaticism at the club with the fans. You could see that, whenever here was a big game or a London derby, or a Millwall derby, my goodness, that's when it really came out on the terraces.

I played in a few games as a West Ham player against Millwall

What was that like?

My goodness! Well, you thought Tottenham was a big derby, and Chelsea and Arsenal at the time. But this was a totally different atmosphere. It was an atmosphere of sheer hatred from both sides. You'd go to the ground and you'd see loads more police, loads more police horses. That was a sign of the magnitude of the fixture for both sets of fans. Then there was the build up to the game and there was no getting away from it. Training was more intense because the players knew how important a game it was. You go out to warm-up and sense the hostility straight away. It was full of hatred. You'd go back in the dressing room and all the talk was, "we've just got to win today, we don't care how, we've just got to win and, heaven forbid, not get turned over.

By the time you come out of the tunnel, you'd hear that deafening noise from the crowd. For me a West Ham v Millwall game always felt like a night game, regardless of what time it kicked-off.

Stick between players?

It wasn't verbal because you couldn't hear it. The atmosphere was just electric. But, my goodness, the tackles would be flying in left, right and centre. Terry Hurlock, he was one for dishing it out. He was one tough cookie and I've heard him called worse! I wouldn't argue with him, but I just wanted to get the ball. My way of not giving any verbals was, "right, he's kicked me and he's hurt me, but I want the ball again. I wanted to take him on again and show him that he didn't intimidate me. So I wanted the ball even more. You could hear the tackles flying in, the elbows, the pinching of the skin, the studs down the back. But that just motivated me to run at them even more.

Different to a normal league game?

Yeah. Obviously it did.

I think it was because of the hooliganism back then. You'd go, "hang on a minute mate, we need to win this because if we got beat and our supporters were getting wound up at Millwall, my goodness, it probably would have kicked off 10 times worse than it did in the streets!"

Is there a particular game you remember?

Yeah, we beat them 3-0 at Upton Park. I had a really good game, and Georgie scored a couple I think. I can remember Bruce Rioch was Millwall manager. I've got a quote from that match where he likened me to Eusebio that day. He said I was the nearest he'd seen to Eusebio that day. And it was against our biggest rivals. I thought, "I'll take that!"

Did trouble in the ground influence players?

From time to time you'd see or hear it kicking off on the terraces, or you'd spot a load of police dashing to one part of the ground or the stewards getting involved. In all honesty it could affect you depending on your character. Some of our players loved it, it brought out the best in them, but I've got to remain tight lipped on that one! That applied to other games like Tottenham and Chelsea as well. You'd think, "the fans are gonna turn here, it's getting a little bit volatile in the terraces, we've got to step it up." You could sense what was going on in the stands.

I was working as an ambassador for the 2009 game against Millwall, and that was the last West Ham - Millwall game at Upton Park. They had the whole of one stand, and the corners by the West Stand and the Chicken Run were left vacant so that they protected the Millwall fans. I remember that night the stadium officer Ronnie Pearce telling us, "It's as much as we can do. He was genuinely worried and he had every right to be because as everyone knows it kicked off very badly night.

When they scored the atmosphere just changed from West Ham being behind us to it becoming so hostile. We were winning comfortable, the fans were cheering and all that, and then Millwall got the equalizer, were a division below us, and then all of a sudden the atmosphere became really tense and it was only a matter of time before it got out of hand. That's how I felt at times when were playing London derbies that, if the result was going well the fans were great and all that, but if it turned or if our performance dipped or they got on top, you could feel the atmosphere change. The tension, and how toxic it could get, you know. There'd be little scuffles in the crowd and you were thinking, "hang on a minute, it's about 50 fans involved at the moment but it could it could become 100's if not 1000's of people getting involved because of the way the game was going on the pitch. So you were thinking, "We better not 2 or 3 down because it'll kick off in the stands.

Celtic - Rangers

When I played in the Old Firm games it is a religion for Celtic and Rangers but having played in both I think West Ham v Millwall would come in that category as well for the fans.

Celtic and Rangers was just massive. Basically you've got 50-60,000. When we played Millwall it was only 25, 30,000 which was half. Yeah, the rivalry was still intense, but London's a big city, with 13 clubs. Whereas when you go Glasgow, there's only two clubs really. So the press build up the magnitude of the game going into it. When you've got a West Ham v Millwall or Tottenham game, it doesn't have the same coverage in the press. But make no bones about it; the intensity is the same, without a doubt. It just probably doesn't get the coverage as what Celtic-Rangers gets in the Scottish press and media up there as what it does down here. And there were only 25,000, I don't know how many the old Den Millwall held, but at Celtic-Rangers you're talking 50-60,000, so it's inevitably a bigger event.

But it was still that intensity. The rivalry, the tackles. We need to win. We *have* to win. The only thing about Celtic and Rangers, because obviously knows you up I Scotland, that if you got beat you probably wouldn't go out for a could f weeks after. With West Ham vs Millwall you could get away with going out just because of the sheer size of London, but you'd still have to be careful if you'd been beat by Tottenham or Millwall. Let's just you probably wouldn't go out on a Saturday or Sunday night if you got beat by either of them two, plus Chelsea I'd throw into that mix.

Don't get me wrong, West Ham fan's love you to bits when you've done well but when you lose in a derby it's, "how can you lose to them?" I never went out after we got beat. I was a boring person. If we did win I would only have a meal or a beer, I wouldn't go out partying or anything like that. I kept my head quite low, i was one of them boring people. I was knackered after the game anyway because of the emotional build-up, and then playing. I'd think, "Jesus, I only want a quiet night." I was lucky. During the week I'd see people at the petrol station and the West Ham fans still be at it. "Of all the teams why couldn't you do them? I don't care about the other teams, that's the game I live for all year, just beat that lot. That'd be mainly Tottenham and Chelsea because we didn't play Millwall that often.

Bill

All the players were aware of the ICF. They had some notorious people. As a player you're aware of that. I was aware of Bill – all the players were aware of Bill because his name used to come up quite a lot among the senior players. As a West Ham fan before he was a West Ham player, Tony Cottee knew a lot of the fans and used to tell us how much respect Bill had among the West Ham fans. I never wet into the politics of it all. I was 31 and I came back to West Ham in the academy because I wanted to be part of this club again. I'd been there from the age of 12-20. I left at 21-22 when I didn't really want to leave. So I had 7 or 8 years away from the Club and my career was becoming a bit too injury prone and I just wanted to come back. So I had a meeting with a meeting Tony Carr. He said, "look Stuart, we'd love to get you back, come and do some coaching with the under 10's-11's in the academy, so I did that. I coached the kids, and they had some good players in there. But the problem a lot of the time was that while the kids were great, it was the parents who were a pain in the backside. Most of them were great but I'd get phone calls after a game. "Stuart he's done well but Chelsea are after my boy and Arsenal are after my boy." I've got all these clubs after my boy is this club going to give him an opportunity?

So one particular evening after I'd had phone calls from irate parents I thought we'll do some coaching but away from the parents. The parents loved watching them and they could hear what I was getting into them. So I pulled them away from the parents right over to the other side from where they were. This was in the evening over at Chadwell Heath, where we had the astro outside under the floodlights.

I'd had enough over the weekend. I was probably on the phone for 3 hours on a Sunday night after a game and all I'm hearing is, "my son could go to Chelsea, my son can go to Arsenal, my son can go to Tottenham. My son's better than West Ham."

So I've pulled them over and I've said, "guys, I've had a few conversations with your parents, and I know you're only young. "But look, you see me, you see the skills that I give you, you see I can still do them. This club was brilliant for me. This club means everything to me. I was small, sleight, skilful, but they believed in me. This club believed in me. this club believed in me more than any other. I owe West Ham United everything, because it gave me a platform. So, rest assured guys, if you're parents think your better than this, that you'd be better off at Chelsea, Tottennham or Arsenal, then go. You can go. Just go.

"But trust me boys, you'd be making a huge mistake. This club, if you're good enough, this club will give you an opportunity. Because it gave me an opportunity, it gave other players an opportunity. It gave players that I played with opportunities. I said, "Chelsea are not gonna give you an opportunity, neither are Tottenham. A boy put his hand up, I looked at him and said, "No, not Arsenal either." Down went his hand. "This is a great club," I continued, ' and in a few years down the road, you'll look back on this time and wonder if your parents made the right decision.

"If you stick with this club and you're good enough, you'll get your chance guys. Because this is a great club, with great supporters, great fans, great people.

"We've got an ethos here. It gives players who have got good technical ability an opportunity. Other clubs don't do that. So forget the Arsenal's, forget the Chelsea's, forget the Tottenham's, forget any other club. You're in a privileged position here. If you're good enough – and trust me you've got to be good enough because there are no guarantees in football - but if you stay and work hard and graft hard, and work like I did, you'll have a chance here.

"I'm giving you the skills that gave me an opportunity. So, you've got loads of time doing 11-a-sides, 5-a-sides, but when you get the opportunity, when you've done your schoolwork, cos your schoolwork is important, when you get an hour don't go on the PlayStation. Do those skills I'm giving you. Do your drills, hone those skills, because is a great opportunity from your age to now go on and get better. Your touch can be better. Your game-perception and game understanding will be better. "

I didn't realise until after the session there was a big fella standing in a part of Chadwell Heath the floodlights didn't reach and where any parents shouldn't have been anyway. He was stood still and seemed to be staring in our group's direction. I got rid of the parents but I was aware – not to mention a little wary – that this very big guy hadn't budged I was half watching the boys going to changed to see their parents. When I looked back round the bloke was walking towards me. He was also getting bigger by the stride. His hands were massive and it actually hurt when he shook mine. I spotted a tattoo on one of his arms. "Bill Gardner," it read. Before I had a chance to ask Bill started speaking. "I know you're West am through and through now. I knew you was West Ham but now I know your West Ham, claret and blue, dyed inn the wool through and through now. I heard your speech, what you said to them kids earlier.

"It was amazing what you told them kids. If that didn't get into them then nothing will; you spoke with passion, desire, and how much this club means so much to you.

His face and hands told me he'd been in a few scraps, but he spoke from the heart. He was obviously West Ham through and through. We ended up having a chat, which us when he told me Ludo was working with his son Dan, one of schoolboy goalkeepers. He's a fanatical fan, he's an absolute die-hard. Loves this club, loves everything about it.
In the time I've got to know Bill since what strikes you is how different he to the character you're always hearing about. For me he's always been an incredibly humble, good guy, you know. People will say things abut him but he comes across so nice, so respectful, always asking about how I'm getting on. And for him to remember that conversation from all those years was amazing,

because it's a great memory I never really forgot even after all these years. We both share a very big importance on trust. It's massively important to both of us.

Trust is a big thing for me growing up because I had that support from my close-knit family, but then you go into the football world and then you go, "oh dear, it's very difficult to trust people. Then there's the press, which I've got a few personal experiences with. And then people in general, you know, the closest to you, they let you down and you don't know who to trust. There were very difficult times, and then when I finished football, you know, where the people that were there when I was in football, all of a sudden there was nobody there. So, trust for me is a huge thing.

Obviously I know about Bill's past. But I don't see that side of him. I can see a humbleness and honesty in him when I've spoken to him. It's very difficult for me to square that perception of him with the one that most people have from those terrace years. I suppose until you've met someone you just form an opinion based on what your told. But to me, Bill's an absolute gentleman who loves his team. Nothing more. Nothing less.

25

Millwall: History and Hatred

For me, they've always been our number one rivals. I've always felt that they were bullies. They always tended to pick on one or two people on their own. I felt destined to hate them with a passion. I don't like Spurs fans, and I'm not a great lover of Man United, but I've got friends at both of those clubs. I've never had a friend at Millwall, however. Historically they are our rivals, dating back to the Thames Ironworks football club in 1895, and that rivalry is alive and kicking.

Whenever we played them, I was at the front, the same as at any other game. Despite my loathing of them, there's a difference between hatred and respect. I give Millwall a great deal of that. They never had as many as us, but they were always game. You can't take that away from them, and I won't lie about that. I used to look around at the faces of a lot of the West Ham supporters around me when we went over there. I always noticed concern in their eyes, which was very rare for our lot. But I could tell.

I never enjoyed going over there myself. It used to get the hairs on the back of my neck up, going over there, and you always knew you were in for a hard day because they always turned up. You knew you were in for a hard time and it wouldn't be a walk in the park over there, you had to be on your best mettle, and most of the time we were. It wasn't a nice place to go, the Old Den. It's easily the worst ground I've ever been to, and the only thing I enjoyed was going through the door and closing it when I got home.

If you were in one piece you'd done well! That's always the way I looked at it.

But that's always the way when we play them.

A lot of West Ham – none of my mates – would mouth off beforehand about what they're going to do over at the old Den, what they aren't going to do, and then wouldn't even show up! You'd hear the feeblest excuses, and I'm talking about West Ham fans. "Oh, I couldn't make it I was ill." I've been ill! I've been ill and I've made it every time, simply because I won't let people down. There were more than a few who let us down, but you live with it.

So yeah, nothing but respect for them. It's a bit like Chelsea. Cass's book came out with a statement I made at Stamford Bridge years ago, and I had that problem with them at Stratford. But I've got loads of Chelsea mates. Nearly all the people who go to watch Corinthian Casuals are Chelsea fans. I get on great with them, and to be fair they've treated me with nothing but respect.

It was a bit out of character what happened at Stratford. There might have been a couple there who knew me, but they weren't the Chelsea people I know and the ones who know me, the top boys, the old guard, however, you want to put it. They were probably kids, but they were annoying fuckers all the same. But like I say, you don't get respect unless you show it, and they showed none at all that night. I've shown respect, and that's what I get back. Once you start stitching people up, or you turn your back on them, or make decisions that aren't in the best interests of the people you're with, you won't get that respect, you'll lose it, and you can lose it real quick.

Billy Neill Testimonial
Millwall – West Ham 1974

We came unstuck a bit that night. Not many West Ham fans went over there for that one, and I was in the middle of the Cold Blow Lane End with Ted, Bunter and Cass. I was looking for their top man 'Tiny', but Millwall surrounded us, and I thought we were going to get a right mullering. The police came in and we went down the stairs and fucked off at half-time. We had to. As I was going down the stairs some geezer comes up the other side and he pulled out a machete. It was unbelievable. I reckon we'd have got done good that night. Somewhere along the line, we got away with it. It was a bad day at the office!

I'm obviously biased, but without doubt, I believe the sheer passion of the hatred between us and them is the biggest in British football. They talk about Celtic and Rangers, Aston Villa and Birmingham, I know that's a big one. I know the Bristol clubs is a bad one, Newcastle and Sunderland that's a bad one, there are loads of them. But Millwall and West Ham is different. There's so much hatred on both sides of the water. I'm a very emotional character, and that lot bring out every emotion I've got.

They're a lot like West Ham fans in their passion, and it's never been personal between us and them. I'll give you an example.

Tiny, the Lion of Millwall

As I've said, Tiny was Millwall's top man. Me and him hated each other more than I can say. More than passionately, let's put it that way. He was my number one enemy. We never did have a row where it was just me and him. We got close to blows a few times, but it never happened. Not on my part, but he was always there. But there was never any, "Come on, me and you, we're both here let's sort this out now." And while I never liked him, I respected him for who he was.

Some years back, around 2010 I think, I received a phone call from a West Ham fan I know who used to help run the West Ham Boxing Club. He was mates with Tiny and was visiting him in hospital. By all accounts, Tiny was in a very bad way and hadn't been given long by the doctors from what I was told. He sadly passed away, but not before we had an emotional phone call from his deathbed.

"Where do you think I am?" my mate asked me on the phone.

"Give up," I replied

"I'm the hospital."

"Are you alright?"

"Nah it's alright, I'm with Tiny."

I went quiet.

"He can't talk. Have you got anything to say to him?"

I was on the spot. I hadn't had any time to think about what to say. Here's a bloke wanting me to speak to my biggest enemy. What do you say to someone who wanted to kill you every time he saw you? With a deep breath I let my mate pass the phone to Tiny.

"Hello Tiny, I'm sorry to hear you're not well. I wish I could help you. We've always been enemies and we always will be, but I will always respect you as Tiny, the Lion of Millwall."

The phone went quiet. My mate got back on and said Tiny was in tears. "It's the first time he's shown emotion in weeks,"

"What, is he upset?" I asked.

"No, he's happy," my mate replied. I showed him respect.

I don't know if he wanted it or if he was coaxed into it by my mate, but what do you say to a man who's dying? "I hope you fucking do die you horrible cunt?" What human being can say that to another in those circumstances? It would've been wrong, and I can live with what I told him.

I felt sorry for him. No one deserves that horrible end, no one. I wanted him to know I had respect for him, and to show that I was bigger than someone who might've cunted him off.

People need to show mercy, compassion, and respect. It's what separates us from the animals. You might get a kick in the bollocks for it, some will let you down and some of them will break your heart. But that's not who you are. You have to be who *you* are in life. Play the game to your rules, not to theirs. I was gutted for the bloke. I don't hate anyone that much that I want to see them die.

I was sorry that the lad went.

I wanted the man to have a respectful end, like he had a respectful life, and that was good enough for me. I didn't know him at all. There was just a bit of shouting and balling between us a few times. But I never took that animosity into civvy street, and as far as I'm aware neither did he. We fronted each other up a couple of times at games, but it never materialised.

Several things come to mind with Tiny, but I won't bad mouth a dead man. It's as simple as that. I didn't like him and he didn't like me, but I can't put down a man who's passed away. I was invited to the funeral, but I didn't want to go because it would've been awkward for me and them. I wasn't frightened of going, but it would have been very awkward for both sides, particularly at a funeral.

A few of us went to the funeral of the wife of a friend of mine. My mate was West Ham, his mates were all West Ham, but her family were all Millwall. Some of their top faces were there, and some of them started getting a little bit silly. I thought to myself, "This is a funeral, we aren't going to have it out at someone's funeral for fucks sake, this is fucking wrong."

I said to the boys, "Look, we're at a funeral here, we can't rare up with these people. We'll show we're bigger than that." And we did. But I tell you what, if we'd still been there 15 minutes after that funeral ended, we'd have fucking upped them because they were bang out of order. A man's lost his wife, they know he's West Ham. I knew her and thought the world of her. He was one of my best mates.

There was no way I was going to start at a funeral, but I'd have been truly tempted to have gone onto the toilet with one of them that day and given him a whooping because they got outrageous with some of their comments and songs. You don't behave like that at a fuckin' funeral. You have a bit of respect.

West Ham v Millwall
Upton Park, 2009

An evening midweek cup game between us and them! Who the fuck thought that was a good idea? They had about 800 fans and the biggest escort I've ever seen. I was down the other end of the road with Carlton, Cass, and a few others because we thought a few might come that way. They didn't. The police marched them from their manor to ours, but by the time they got to Upton Park station, there was thousands waiting for them. It all went off at the station and in the side streets. There were paving stones being wedged out and broken up to sling at them, which was never for me. I didn't know until afterwards what went on. I got home and saw it on TV. But, yeah, it was a lively night, that's for sure. A lot of the locals come out that night and I do believe the police saved their lot from a serious bashing.

I know that when they come round the corner from the station they were well concerned. They'll say they weren't, but they were. As cautious as we were over their place, they were always cautious coming to Upton Park. I won't say any more on that one. But they know, they know. A lot of them shit themselves that night, and I don't blame them to be fair. It was crazy. A madhouse.

I wasn't involved that night. I was in a hurry to get in that night as well, so I didn't hang about. But nothing happened down where we were. I went by car, so down where I was standing, I had a parking space. So, I never went near the railway station in any way, shape, or form that night.

It seemed to be pretty spontaneous in fairness. Everyone heard the trains were fucked, they'd stopped the District line and it was madness in central London as a result. Word got round and all of a sudden people were saying let's go up the station. That could mean anything. But I didn't know too much about it to be fair.

A few of them took a clump or two, so I heard. Someone got stabbed I think but I just heard somebody got done.

Why Millwall?

Because they're our biggest rivals. I can only answer it like that. It's because they are. I think 90 percent of West Ham fans will say Tottenham are our biggest rivals, but it'll never be Tottenham in front of Millwall for me.

When they got in trouble and there was talk of them going out of business or moving to Kent, I hated it. I want them to do well, get themselves in the Premier League so we can play them again. I'm the last person in the world who wants Millwall to go out of business, believe me. When we got knocked out of the league cup last year and it turned out we would have been drawn to play Millwall in the next round I was gutted. Truly gutted.

I'm too old now at any rate, and those days have maybe passed me by. My uncle died racing a Millwall fan to the khasi on his Zimmer frame. They bumped into each other, my uncle went down and he died. It was an accident, a joke that backfired, so I haven't got any love for them. I've got respect for them, but no love. They know where they stand with me. That's the way it's always been. I've never lost that feeling towards them. They know that themselves. If you ask them truthfully, they'll probably tell you they hate me more than any other West Ham supporter because they can't bully me, I don't take a backward step and I don't take shit off of them.

26

Tough

By the late '70s and early '80s West Ham could put more lunatics on the road than any other club in England. That's not boasting. It's a fact. We had more nutters than any other club, loads more and they were genuine, fighting people. There was a stage where at a push we could have put 7,000 on the road. Nutters. All nutters. At least 7,000 absolute lunatics who cared about nothing except West Ham and our reputation. We didn't have the biggest crowds, we didn't have the Manchester United or Newcastle crowds, but when the shit hit the fan, West Ham always turned up.

I talk to my mates and they go on about this bloke and that bloke who I've never met but who were active in them days. It's makes me think, 'Christ almighty, how many were there?' At some away games there'd be 1500, 2000, up for it to a man. No stragglers. No hangers on. That was home or away. It was unbelievable, and I always think that was the reason why we were the best.

West Ham Pride

The East End of London can be an unforgiving place. But it's also a place full of history and tradition. West Ham United is central to that identity. The area, the war, the blitz, the dockers, the violence. All those things come into play when you talk about having pride in the Club. It's all part of the melting pot that makes us who we are. Let's get it right; every teams got its tough people. Every single team. You could go to the tiniest outposts like Dunstable, non-league clubs like Folkestone, small teams like Doncaster. Lincoln in the Milk cup in 1982, was a tough old night.

But we had more people, and there was that pride. A feeling in people's chest. "I'm West Ham." The trust that they had in each other that, if they went over, somebody would pick them up. Somebody would look after them. Other teams didn't have that. Tottenham have never had that. I've spoken to Tottenham fans and it's a load of different groups. But if one shits themselves, the other ones start to. There's no unification between any of them. Once you get unification between large groups of people you can stand alone. West Ham always stood alone.

It was a truly unique thing. It showed what British people are all about. We do stick together, but some more than others.

We weren't the only ones. There were plenty of them like Millwall, Chelsea, Birmingham, Villa, City, Manchester United, every club had this group of fans that were up for it. It was like a league table and West Ham was top of the league. It's the only thing we had in the bloody trophy cabinet. We never won much on the pitch!

Top Firms?

As I say no one could touch us in those days. In no order, based on my personal experience I'd mention teams like Derby, Forest, Stoke, Millwall, the Geordies, Middlesbrough, Sunderland, Southampton. Southampton may surprise a few people but in the

'70s they had a right mix of people; they had a load of dockers and farmworkers who used to come in for the game. They didn't mind a row. I suppose it's better than sheep-shagging! There was always a little turn out down there.

But nothing was easy. You treated everyone with respect and saw how you got on. Like I say, we always had more. Where they might have a group of 20, 3 might want to have a go, 10 didn't want to know and 7 would if they had to. In our group of 20, 19 would be frothing at the mouth. Always. That made it a different ballgame altogether.

I've been fortunate. I've known some great people over there. I've loved being with a lot of them. Some of them not so much, but most of them I'd say were great people. I just hope that when I go, they don't forget me, and they come and see me go down the last route. When I die, I'd like them to come to my funeral. I'd like all of them to come, even my enemies. Because I gave them respect, I'd like to think they've got the class to give the respect back. I'd like to think there'd be no bother. Just football fans standing together.

27

Joey Williams (The Mile End Mob)

By the time Joey Williams was eleven years old he was making his money by washing the cars of Ronnie and Reggie Kray at their Wentworth nightclub in Bethnal Green.

The vehicle interior would regularly be teeming with money clips containing hundreds of coins acquired through a Central London parking meter scam. As Joey freely admits, temptation often got the better of him, and a few money clips were often significantly lighter after he'd left work for the day.

In later years one of London's most talked about fights of the day would involve Joey and Lenny McLean at the White Swan pub near Cable Street in Wapping, where McLean was a doorman.

As Joey recalls, "He kept going for me with his truncheon, so I took it off him, gave him a smack and he toed it inside the club.

I waited outside for him with his truncheon in my hand to settle it, but he never came out."

"People call everyone mate these days, but back then it meant something. It was important. Bill was my mate, my friend. He knew he could rely on me, and I knew I could rely on him.

Bill meets his old mate Joey Williams for the first time in 47 years
(Photo by Nigel Tufnell)

"I first saw him at Mile End Station in 1968 or 1969. He was young, but you could tell he could look after himself. He was like us - he wasn't frightened of anybody. I can't explain it any other way.

'The late '60s was when football started for us. It was just something that we really wanted to do. Fight other firms from other teams.

We'd been rowing with other firms all over London by then anyway, like when we had to go over to Bethnal Green once to sort some firm out, but that was nothing to do with football.

Unless you were from the manor, from Mile End, you couldn't be in the Mob. Simple as that. You were an outsider.

We had a few stragglers and hangers-on back then. There were a few from Stepney and Bow who'd knock about with us.

Bill understood how things worked. He wasn't from Mile End. But more than anyone else from outside the manor, the Mob took to Bill.

But he was far from some straggler or hanger-on. He was a tough man, a brave man. But like I say most of all he was, he is, my mate.

I could go over West Ham today, say, "Hello Bill," and he'd shake my hand. I always knew if I went steaming in, he'd be behind me. He was never scared, he wasn't scared of anyone, and he wasn't scared of us.

We all backed each other up, and there was no way in the world you'd not fight for our mob. If you were in it, you'd have to throw punches. Because if you didn't, and you toed it, you'd have got murdered.

You'd have got a right good hiding off of us, never mind the other lot. Then you'd be blanked and you'd never be allowed back in. It happened to a few lads.

But Bill was always there. He was never shy when it came to having a row. He liked to be in with the action, and he could have a proper fight, I'll tell you.

When you're looking at people and you're in a situation where you need people to back you up, he'd be there. He wanted to be there. I'm glad I know the man.

I remember one game at Coventry in the early '70s. We [the Mile End Mob] were in their end having it with them.

A West Ham fan has come steaming over to Bill and gone, "Bill, look, there's a load of Coventry there, let's do them." Bill looked at who he was pointing at and it was us! This fella didn't know who was who.

"Nah, you're on your own there, mate," Bill said to him. I had a good chuckle at that.

As far as I knew, at that time, Bill was in the TBF, who we respected because they were a mob that was willing to fight for West Ham.

At West Ham all the gangs, mobs, crews, whatever you want to call them, they came together. It made us such a powerful firm, though to be fair none of the other West Ham firms were as vicious as us.

We'd help other West Ham supporters at away games if they backed us up, but to be honest, we just wanted to fight these football firms across the country. End of. Either you were with us or you were in the way. We went where we wanted and did what we wanted.

The Mile End Mob

The Mob started up in the mid-60's. My family lived right behind Mile End station for three years before we had to move to Poplar, when one of the ceilings came down. The mob was just a crew of geezers.

We never really had a leader. We didn't need one. Everybody had their suggestions based on what they'd heard was being said about us. If we heard about another firm mugging us off, saying they could slap us about, we'd go over to their manor and slap them about.

We never went to West London, but we'd heard there was a firm in Ladbroke Grove who were coating us off, so we made an exception, went over there, and sorted them out. That's how it was back then. There were gangs and firms all over London and it was always going off. That side of it was more about our firm, to be honest. But we took that mentality with us over to Upton Park and across the country with West Ham.

The Mile End Mob & West Ham United

My brother Paul first introduced me to football. He was staunch West Ham all his life. He went to a private school because he wasn't well. He had asthma, eczema, and he used to go to a boarding school in Woodford.

I naturally followed him, and 95 percent of the manor was West Ham; just because of the area. But there were a couple of boys in the firm who weren't Hammers.

One of them was Vicky Hardy. He was an Arsenal supporter. But, because he was with us, because he was from the manor, he was part of our mob.

Mind you, he went to West Ham more than he ever went to Arsenal! The only time he ever went to Arsenal was with us!

The Rise and Demise of the Mile End Mob

Rise

There was a club across the road from Mile End station called the A Train. It was one of those soul clubs, and people used to come from all over London to go there.

A lot of them were Jamaicans and they always used to go down there. We started going there and we just used to row with them all the time. I'd have been about 16, 17.

I think that's more or less when it started, the Mob. From then on when we used to have regular rows in that club.

We'd always gather in the same place, go into the club and smash fuck out of it. We had black mates with us, on our side, because they were from the manor, which meant they were part of our gang.

It was all about different manors back then, you know. To us, if you weren't from Mile End but on our patch, you were an outsider and fair game. End of.

After that we used to go to loads of different places. We'd go to south London, anywhere there was a chance of a row, we'd go.

It's not like we were protecting the manor. We didn't have to. I mean who the hell would want to come to Mile End and start a row with us? They'd have got murdered, fucking murdered.

Mile End was safe back then. It was for me. I was never worried about nothing. The only people I was bothered about was the Old Bill.

Demise

One bonfire night in the late '70s, we went to Trafalgar Square to bash Millwall. They were supposed to be meeting us. The meet was set for a row. Just the Mile End Mob, but we had a lot of stragglers with us then.

Anyway, they never turned up. A few of us waited a bit while a few others got on the tube at Charing Cross to go home on the underground, when someone recognised a mate of mine called Dennis.

Dennis was a goalkeeper with a lot of mouth. We used to play football with teams south of the water. One of that lot, I think they were from Eltham, recognised Dennis and a big fight started in the station.

A few people got stabbed in the fight, and something like four to six weeks later the Old Bill come round and picked us up, saying you were part of the mob that stabbed these kids.

Dennis got nicked and did a stretch for that, if I remember rightly.

After that everyone started drifting away from the mob. It sort of started dying. But we stayed mates and good friends. I still see loads of my mates from that time now and again at West Ham.

None more so than Bill, whose love and support of West Ham goes back so long, and whose bravery has saved the bacon of many a Hammer down the years.

28

Collier Row

I have loads of great mates in the ICF. But Mile End was the best firm we ever had. The ICF was more organised than the Mile End, had some good lads and more of them. However, man for man, they couldn't touch the Mile End. While Mile End probably only numbered 80 or 90 lads, every one of them could have a tear-up. A proper tear-up. Not just running in and slapping someone and running away. I mean damage. They didn't give a fuck. It's probably why Mile End didn't have a lot of respect for other West Ham firms. It was their way or the highway. That said, if they respected you, they were the best people to have around bar none.

Was That a Lager or a Luger?
I come from Hornchurch, and on a Friday night we used to go to a place called Kings Hall, which is down by the Romeo Corner. There used to be a large gang in there, 100, maybe 150-strong from Collier Row. A couple of my mates from Rainham had gone in there the week before and got a good hiding. One nearly lost his eye. So, we said we'll go down there the next week and have it out with them. There were about 12 of us. Any rate, we've gone down there, but there were far too many. The

following week I phoned up the Mile End boys. I said, "Look, I need your help." I spoke to Joey Williams, who is, without doubt, one of the toughest people I've ever met. He came up with about 15 or 20 lads. As they came out of the station at Elm Park, one of them put something in my hand and said, "There you go, Bill." I looked down and there was a fucking Luger in my hand. A loaded fucking Luger. I said, "I don't want that." He said, "I thought we was gonna kill them." I said, "No we ain't, it's a row, that's all it is."

Three of us reached the King's Hall - me, Joey, and a boy called Martin Clark (aka Spider). We said to him, "When the record stops, you turn off the lights. When it starts up again, you turn the lights back on." Me and Joey were stood at the bar when the song started to fade out. We both put our drinks on the counter and Spider's turned off the lights. Me and Joey just steamed into them. As soon as the music started up again, up went the lights. It was pandemonium. The blokes were cursing, and the women were screaming. At any rate, the next record starts fading out and Spider does it again. Me and Joey steamed in again before the next song started and the lights went back on. I nearly got rumbled because I was trying so hard not to laugh. They were all having a go at each other trying to work out who the fuck was clumping them in between songs, and who the fuck was turning the lights on and off? We did it twice more until they sussed out it was us. We left sharpish as the Collier Row firm chased us out. The rest of the Mile End was across the road, laying behind some gravestones at the cemetery opposite. As Collier Row has come out, Mile End stood, went across the road, and just murdered them. I mean proper done 'em. We kicked their arses all the way down to Romeo Corner. It probably doesn't sound it, but it was an unbelievably funny night. I was young, 16, I think. Joey's a bit older than me, I think he was maybe 18 or 19 at the time. But he's still about, and I'd like to wish him well. They were a ferocious gang; the Mile End Mob. They were also very good boys and great friends.

29

Palermo

When we got to our hotel we went a night after the trouble. The trouble had all been the night before. We arrived during the day, so we heard all about what happened the night before. Our boys were attacked, they were outnumbered, they fought back and the Italians didn't it. It's as simple as that. You've got to remember we never backed off from anybody, ever. Nor did the Palermo mob. They had a right go, they was totally outnumbered, even the old Bill was against them. There were stories of the Italians throwing hot olive oil from the flats on top of our boys. It was like something out of a fucking medieval castle siege.

One of my best mates Jock, he got hit with a scaffold pole, Ted got hurt, and about 60 West Ham fans got arrested in one night. That's quite big for one night. When we got there and got to our hotel, we obviously wanna go and meet the lads. Our hotel was double booked. We had no end of rows with the manager, we said we'd set fire to his office if he didn't give us what we'd paid for. He found us another place quite a way of Palermo, so about 70 of us were pushed in different hotels.

I was with John Waddell, his brothers, I think big Neil was with us. My mate Neville Bolton was with us. We checked into this hotel a bit outside Palermo, and we wanted something to eat.

I felt more angry about not being there that night when the boys needed me than I felt when the trial ended. I wasted 16 weeks and my family were worried shitless about everything, but not being there that night, not putting a shift in to help them lads, that hurt more.

We'd heard there'd been some trouble, but we didn't know to what degree. When we got there we didn't know what we was going to be facing.

When we marched to the ground together on the night of the game it was women and kids on the inside so they'd have less chance of getting hurt. Italians were pouring hot cooking oil over us from the flats. I got a bit in my mouth and remember thinking, "olive oil, and lovely."

I looked ahead and saw Ray Winstone walking towards the ground. When the scooters started coming with the pillion rider slashing West Ham fans, I looked up again and Ray had disappeared. I looked round and all of a sudden he was behind me.

"Not like it is in the films, eh mate," I said to him. He's a good bloke Ray, a very, very passionate West Ham. Talking to him time that night was the only time I cracked a laugh, because I was already thinking about the trip back to the hotel after the game. We were fighting their fans and the local Old Bill.

We'd had the same sort of thing years ago in Madrid when we played Castilla. West Ham fans just watching game were attacked by the Spaniards.

30

Protection

I would either fight at football or when I was working on the door in the clubs. Even then I used to give people so many chances that they could walk away. People used to say to me, "You give them too many chances," but I think I was fair. I think I'm a fair bloke. I've never been a bully and I've never liked bullies.

When it came to other firms having a dig at West Ham fans, it was always a strange feeling for me. I felt these lads are my family and I've got to look after them. I felt that these people want to hurt my family. I never had anything against anyone because they supported Manchester United, Chelsea, Liverpool, or Millwall.

It's *never* been about the team they support. It's about how they are to my family. I could never stand here and watch a West Ham fan getting a good hiding.

Something inside me says this isn't going to happen. Something tells me you mustn't let this happen. He's my mate, my family if you like, even if I didn't know them. I've had it before. I had it in Manchester years ago in 1973. I was on a coach with my first Mrs, Leslie. We were going to Blackpool afterwards. In those days there used to be a big car park behind the Kippax, which was the main home end at Man City. Away supporters' team coaches used to park there.

I went back to the coach after the game and there was a big fight starting. Our coach was pretty full and two West Ham boys were fighting four Man City fans. The West Ham lads weren't doing too well to be fair; the Manchester City boys were giving them a good hiding, so I steamed in. I whacked a couple of them, and I thought the two blokes I was helping would get up and help me.

But they didn't. They got up and fucked off back on the coach! Nobody got off. The only one who tried to get off to help was Leslie! I broke my finger whacking one of them, we went to Blackpool afterwards, and I ended up in Rush Green Hospital early on a Sunday morning getting my finger done up.

31

Danny Brown (Aston Villa)

As a person, Bill is no-one's fool. He's not an idiot. You can tell he's a tough guy, but I would describe him as a gentleman who knows how to speak to people.

He's not the kind of geezer you'd want to cross, but at the same time is very well informed and says it as it is. That's how I view Bill.

The late '70s and early '80s were rough times, there's no getting away from that. Being a Villa fan was no different. I mean to say, you stayed with your lot. But when I started going to Villa, I was a scarfer, I wasn't attracted to the violence. That came later.

I went to Villa Park for the football. But when you saw what was going on and how it worked, it's something you kind of just get into, especially as a teenager. Not everybody's cup of tea perhaps, but it was for a fair few.

A Day Out in London

West Ham United away in the quarter-final of the FA Cup. It was Spring 1980 and I was about to experience my first encounter with Bill Gardner.

Or at least I think I did.

I'll never be 100 percent sure because, almost 40 years later, that day went into Villa folklore where it remains. It was a real learning experience for us.

By the time that game came around, we'd been to places like Cambridge and Blackburn, got off the coach, and just smashed everyone and everything in our way to pieces. I would've been about 17 or 18 at the time.

When we drew West Ham away in the quarter-final I thought, "Yeah, we'll go up there and cause havoc, follow the Old Bill on the way out and we'd be sorted."

Big mistake.

Our coach arrived in an East London side street a few hours before kick-off, close to the old away end at Upton Park. A few of us thought we'd go looking for a few of West Ham's main lads.

So, we set off thinking a few more Villa would join us, given how close it was to the away end. All of a sudden, we spotted these West Ham lads. They were men. Big, grown men! Before we'd had the chance to say, "Who are these fuckers?" we were under attack.

Being honest, it was a nightmare. We'd gone down there looking for it, but this was a mismatch, pure and simple.

It didn't get any better once we were in the ground either. There was a lot of trouble in the Villa End that day.

Us youngsters at the front were doing alright to be fair but I got dragged out by the Old Bill who marched me all the way past West Ham's Chicken Run stand.

They were lobbing all sorts at me, cups of tea, meat pies. I saw West Ham fans trying to break through the police lines to get to me.

But something was happening in the Villa End that day that I'd never seen before. The West Ham lads looked like an army in their green bomber jackets. They would steam into our older lads at the back of the stand, kick-off hard, then they'd just vanish; like completely gone.

The West Ham lads looked like an army in their green bomber jackets. They just kept steaming into our end, kicking-off, then disappearing again.

It was more than just a few of us taking a slap. It was more psychological than that. It was the waiting for them to come back in that killed us. We didn't know when the next wave of attacks would be. Somehow, they just kept coming in and out, again and again.

We tried having it with them but, like I say, it was a mismatch. We just couldn't work out how they kept getting in and out of the away end so easily.

I would later, however, hear a story about that day which still does the rounds at Villa Park today. I don't know if it's true, but it goes like this:

A West Ham fan had control of one of the doors leading from the streets to the terraces at our end of the ground that day.

He'd been letting the West Ham firm in and out of the ground all through the game, before leading them onto the terraces and into the Villa End.

As the story went, that man's name was Bill Gardner, and he was supposed to be West Ham's top man. That's what the Villa boys I looked up to told me, so as far as I was concerned, it was true.

That's how I discovered who Bill Gardner was, years before I met him. To this day, I don't know if that story is true or not. I would later ask him and he smiled in response before changing the subject.

Take from that what you will. In fairness, Bill could deny it and it wouldn't change a thing. That was what happened. End of. That was the official line doing the rounds in our part of Birmingham and beyond.

Looking back, I don't suppose it matters who did what on that day, but Bill's name was on the lips of almost every Villa fan in the immediate aftermath of that game, and a piece of terrace folklore erupted into reality.

It became a famous story of the time, and everybody at Villa speaks about that game because it was one of those moments when reality hits you.

Not every away game's going to be like Cambridge or Blackburn, where we could just turn up and roll people over. West Ham that year was a reality check.

We were teenagers and these were blokes in their 20's. When you're in your teens and facing grown men, it's a different ballgame.

I met Bill a few times years later, once at Cass's 50th birthday party. I went down to London, and it was an absolute pleasure meeting Bill in person. Cass introduced him to me and I just thought to myself, "He looks like he can handle himself!"

He was just a proper geezer. So much so that it didn't seem the right time or place to ask him about that game in 1980.

Bill and I also received parts in Cass's film, which was a great experience. It was like a who's who of the top boys from across the country's top firms.

When Bill arrived on the set, you knew about it. You felt his presence, and you could see from the faces and greetings from the other lads just how widely respected he was.

I think a lot of that respect was down to the fact that the top boys knew Bill as a lone figure; a leader and not a follower. He wasn't ever really seen with any firms or any of the main faces we knew about.

When Bill Met Dennis

I invited Cass down to one of the boxes at Villa Park for a game against West Ham around 2005. He agreed to come up but then had some business to take care of with the director of his movie so couldn't do it. So, I said to him, "You know what would be cool if we could get Bill to come instead."

I've become good friends with Cass over the years, and added, "I'm not being funny Cass, but getting Bill Gardner up here would be bigger than having you here!"

Cass gave me his number and all the arrangements were made. I told the Corporate team at Villa, "Cass can't come, but let's get Bill Gardner." They were like, "You know Bill Gardner! Bloody hell!" Everyone was buzzing.

Bill brought his boy with him, but it got ridiculous in the executive box. He was surrounded by loads of people just wanting to say hello and shake his hand. Everyone knew who he was.

I then witnessed the most surreal thing ever. Dennis Mortimer, Aston Villa's legendary European-cup winning captain, asked if he could shake Bill's hand! And he did!

I was there and saw it with my own eyes. Dennis Mortimer knew all about Bill. I guess that's what they mean when they say Bill's name transcended the terraces.

Watching the two of them shaking hands I sort of looked away, shaking my head. I was pretty shocked, and it takes a lot to shock me. But seeing one of our all-time greats shaking hands and chatting with Bill, it sort of blew away a little bit.

It was like being a little kid again. I was just thinking, "There's no way anyone's going to believe me when I tell them this!" But it happened. No bullshit.

He was just a top geezer with everyone at Villa that day. Just the way he was, his character, the way he spoke to people.

Bill Gardner the Man

Certain names are just connected to certain teams and always will be. Bill Gardner's name will always be connected to West Ham United in the eyes of football supporters across the country and further.

As far I was concerned, yeah, he had a reputation. I certainly considered him West Ham's top man. I think a lot of it was to do with the fact he was more of an individual than part of any firm. A lot of people think that he was part of the ICF.

To be honest, that's what I thought until I got to know him. When you think back, it makes sense. It was never 'Bill Gardner with the ICF'. It was always him on his own.

When you remember all the things the ICF got up to, Bill's name was never mentioned in connection with any of them. We knew the faces, we knew the names. But when the stories about what the ICF had been up to came out, Bill's name was never mentioned.

I can only make one conclusion – Bill wasn't with them at the time these things were happening. Next thing I know his name's all over the papers and he's on trial for being the ICF's top man.

That didn't make any sense to me at all. West Ham's top man, maybe, but never the leader of a firm.

Looking back on the history of terrace culture in Britain, I'd have to say that, in and around the 1980s, Bill Gardner was probably its most important figure. One hundred percent. In fairness, it's probably also true in my opinion that West Ham was the toughest firm of that era.

For all that, you never saw Bill. You knew who to look out for and for me he was the ultimate. But there were a few times the ICF kicked off somewhere and, as I've said, Bill's name was never mentioned. So it's not just about toughness for me. It's about that presence, that leadership.

Bill was nobody's fool. He knew his stuff football-wise, talk about how teams set-up, their strengths, and weaknesses. I've been told by a few at West Ham he would've made a top manager, even before I knew one of his boys was the manager at Corinthian Casuals and the other their keeper.

I'll talk to Bill about a few topics aside from football and the old days. He's an intelligent man.

But I draw the line at speedway. I know he's a big speedway fan, but for me, it's just more noise than I need in my life. But in the grand scheme of things, and with all the water that's gone under the bridge, it's probably not something worth falling out over now!

It may sound a cliché, but I've always had a lot of respect for West Ham fans. A little later in life, I moved down south for work and was surrounded by them.

It's a tough area, the East End of London always felt like it had an edge to it. As for me, I was well on my way up the ranks at Villa, and it's fair to say I was a known entity within football.

So, when the bloke I was sharing digs with down south, a mad West Ham fan, kept offering me tickets to go down to Upton Park for a home game, I'd have to come up with every excuse in the book.

Every other weekend the whoppers got bigger. I was either fixing a motor - which I didn't even have! – or going round mates when they were all in Birmingham!

I just couldn't risk going to Upton Park. This was around the mid-eighties and by then I was well acquainted with the people to look out for.

I was on a good thing with work, and there was no point getting spotted. It just wasn't worth the risk.

I told Bill that story years later, when he and Cass arranged safe passage for me and my mates from Kings Cross to Upton Park, before taking us out on the town after a game.

He pissed himself when I told him that. "Maybe I should make up for lost time," he said with a big grin. That's Bill all over for me, a fantastic gentleman and a top geezer.

32

Enemies

I think I've got a lot of people who don't like who I am or what I am. But I can't change their thinking, and they can't change mine. I personally have not got one person that I hate that much. There's a lot of people who I dislike immensely, for one thing and another, but I can get through life without hating somebody. I don't have to hate them. But football's a massive part of my life. I'm a passionate man, and I'm passionate about my football. There's a lot of people that are passionate about their footfall, and there's a lot that just give and take it.

A lot of people don't have that passion. Win or lose they go home and couldn't give a shit. When West Ham lose – which was and is a lot of the time – there's no point being around me. When we played Millwall and Christian Dailly put the ball into his own net during that 4-1 drubbing - let's get it right they took the piss out of us that day, I went home, was in bed by 8 o'clock, and if I'd had a cat I'd have kicked it right up the arse.

I went to bed, got the covers over my head, and just wanted to forget the day. I know I'll get stick for letting that out of the bag; but it's true. It was one of the worst days of my life. To lose like that to them. I think they made Dailly their player of the year which I thought was funny. They've done a couple of funny things over the years. When we were at Wigan, they had the airplane go over didn't they, 'Avram Grant - Millwall legend' - I creased up. I thought that was as funny as hell. You've got to have a sense of humour. As much as things were naughty in those days - and still can be occasionally - to have a sense of humour is a good thing to have.

I don't know how people see me. I like to think that people say that Bill's a nice fella, he's quite funny, he's loyal, but he won't be fucked about with. That's how I want to be remembered. I don't want people to say, Bill Gardner, he was a hard bastard, because I truly don't believe that I was. I was being me.

Certain things get stretched. I did a few things that maybe I shouldn't have done, a few things that were a bit silly and looking back absolutely ridiculously stupid. Some people might interpret them as being brave but looking back now, I think I'd interpret them as being a bit silly. But these rumours get around. Nottingham Forest was a good example. Where once I may have thought I'd done well, I now think what nutter walks toward the other firm with bricks and lumps of wood bouncing off him? It certainly wasn't good for my health!

But I've only ever had one gear - forward. There's no reverse with me. That's the way it is. But things do get pulled out of proportion, and anyone who's been in the same position as me at any club, they know what I mean when I say things get stretched. I mean front markers, rather than backmarkers. We had plenty of backmarkers. I've seen them. I've seen them gradually slipping further and further back. Nobody ever saw me slip back, that's for sure. It's not in my nature and I ain't a good runner

A lot of the people from that time I would have called my enemies. And they know that, because, at the end of the day, I was only the one, out of all the clubs, who was at the front without fail. Despite what some muppets have put up in their books, I never knew them. If I had have done, I'd say so. I've named a few people in here – with their permission – who were the real deal. I might not have rated their firms, but I can say they were tough, tough men. But as for the rest of them, I never had anyone who's a 'name' come up to me, introduce themselves, and say, "Come on, me and you now." Never, and they know that. But they know I was there. There's no excuse in saying, "I weren't there." I was always there. Always at the front with the same people who have been at the front every single year of my life. The same great mates that I've had who are now getting on in life, but still got that pride in themselves, and that fight in their belly.

33

New Definitions of a Hard Man

I've lost count of the times I've been asked who's the toughest man I've come up against. My answer's always the same.

How do you determine what's hard? Do you term hard by a person who's a fighter, a person like myself whose boxed, done tae-kwon-do, a bit of karate, and liked wrestling? Or do you talk about the person that would stand by you and never leave you, even though he was terrified and couldn't hold his hands up. I've had plenty stand alongside me who I knew were terrified. But I could see they were never, ever gonna leave me. And yet they'd never had a fight in their life. So, as far as that goes, enough said. The hardest person I've met would be the man or woman who gets up at 4 o'clock in the morning to go to work to feed his or her three kids on low wages. They're tough people.

As far as football fans go, I never rated none of them. None of them was ever at the front when they've said they were looking for me. It's funny how the ones who say they were, weren't, and the ones who don't talk about it were. The ones with big mouths all say this and that, but they were never there, and they *know* they were never there. I don't need to say who they are, and I wouldn't want to embarrass them. They can manage that without any help from me. To coin a phrase I've used all my life, 'they was two bob, the lot of them'.

For years people have gone on about this gang, that gang, this mob from this team, that firm from that team. But in my experience, very few of the people that put themselves at the top of the tree could actually have a proper fight. A lot of it was about steaming down the road, throwing chairs, throwing bricks, everyone jumping on one person. When it came to actual violence I saw very few people who could, or would, stand there and have it. I mean proper have it. Where they get punched in the mouth and their teeth come flying out, the blood starts flying out, and they laugh and get stuck in again.

I saw very few people like that from any club. I read these 'hard man' books and watch these 'hard man' films and think, "How comes I was always at the front and I don't remember you?" I think a lot of them have massive egos, that have to be fed with a load of bullshit. And people that were with me know that I was never a backmarker. I was always at the front. Our lot knew that I could have it. I was a fighting man and I would not back away, or back down. I never have and I never will. A lot of today's firms I call the slap and tickle brigade; they're like bees on honeycomb. One person puts up a fight and once the fight starts all of a sudden their mates will jump on top of him. That's what it's been like since the end of the eighties. I've met some very good lads at West Ham who could have a row. But not many of the other teams did.

Babs from Chelsea, yeah he was alright. Tiny from Millwall, he could have it because you have to have something about you to be the top man over there. They're like us, they've got old, and the older you get you start to mellow. But back then there was a bit of excitement in it, as the adrenaline raced through our bodies. But every morning I wake up, that chapter of my life's another 24-hours further back in time. Now I just get on with my life and enjoy what I can, when I can, how I can. I think that's what a lot of the older boys do at a few clubs. The one thing I think we have in common is we've all got mutual respect for each other. We don't live in each other's pockets and we don't like kissing arse. But what we do have is respect for the past and for each other.

I don't like talking about some of the old characters at other clubs because I want to do everyone justice. If I name one, he might not be half as hard as somebody else. But like I say, for me, I look at a person very differently to others in that respect. Some people might look at someone and say, "Oh he's a mug," or "he's two bob," but I look at the person that can't fight, that will be by my side till the bitter end. That's a hard person, because what they're doing isn't natural to them. A fighting man's totally different. I had the opportunity to name name's when I did the 'Hard Bastards' book and 'On the Terraces'. But I did those for my mate, Cass, because I wanted to help him out as best I could. We've been mates for a long while. We're still mates now. At one time Cass was made out to be the big bad wolf among a few of the lads at West Ham, and once again the sheep all followed. But I saw through it. Life's a big test. It's a big test of survival. Do you believe what some friends are saying about other friends? A lot of things were said about him, and there's things that he knows I feel quite strongly about, particularly when it comes to saying too much about certain things. But I can never blame a man for trying to do the best for his family. He's always tried to do the best for his family, and me and him will always be good friends.

34

John Wraith (QPR)

I first met Bill when I was about 16 years old and he was the head doorman at Busby's nightclub in Redhill. He was still married to Jan at the time. This was about 35 years ago. I was young then, but old enough to know who Bill Gardner was at that time.

He was very well known and in his prime. I'm not sure how long he'd been living in the Woodhatch (Reigate/Redhill manor), but being a little bit of a scoundrel myself, we did a couple of little scams on the doors years ago. Busby's was a big deal, like a super club, in a time when there weren't many big clubs like that. It would attract a lot of people down from London to it.

These were the days when you used to have a blazer and tie to get in. There always used to be a big queue to get in, so I used to go along the queue and collect a few quid off the punters and then go to open the fire doors and let a load in that way and then paid my dues to Bill!

They were good old days on the doors.

I played for Woodhatch for many years, the team which Bill managed. The players from those days have kept a strong link, which remains still today. That was because of Bill. Through the nucleus of the team having the utmost respect for Bill. We were all a lively little group of lads.

Bill always looked after us, all the way through. Bill's one of those people who always kept an eye on you, looked after you and always had your best interests at heart. Most of us are still friends now and still keep in contact, I think he's always had the father-son relationship with us, if you know what I mean.

Bill's got the kindest heart in the world. He's just one of those people. His persona, his presence, his bottle, that's what made him a true leader. He's got the kindest heart, he doesn't suffer fools easy, and I mean Bill's charismatic beyond belief. He's funny, he's kind, he would always do anything for you. If it was in Bill's power to help you, he would.

I ended up working for him doing driveways and patios and everything. I worked for him on and off. So, he's been a large figure in my life, basically, from late teens to this day.

I don't know if I needed it, but he was certainly someone that I could look up to when I lost my doorman license.

Charisma

Whenever you're in Bill's company he holds court, because he is a naturally funny person. But also, he's a listener. He's not someone that wants to take over every conversation. He always shows an interest in what you're doing; what you're talking about. Even if you go long periods and haven't spoken, at the back of his mind he's always looking out for you, and sometimes you don't even know it!

I was living in Thailand at the time of the first massive tsunami. I was in a bar at the time it hit the other side of the country, so I didn't know anything about it. My phone went, and it was Bill. He was the first person who phoned me to see if I was OK was. I didn't even know there's been a Tsunami. I was half thinking, "What's he talking about?" I also thought, "How does he know I'm in Thailand?"

As we spoke word was coming through about the tsunami on the news.

He never forgets people, so now and then I like to give him a call to see how he's getting on. Bill's had, over the years, his fair share of scrapes and little bits of trouble and I'd like to think I've always been there or offered to be there for him as well.

When they got arrested, I took Sarah to court every day. I lost my job over it, to be honest. I was taking Sarah, in Bill's car, up to Snaresbrook every day, then he got moved to the nick so I was driving her to Brixton.

That's when I met a few of the other boys like Cass. I made friends with a good few of them and we've stayed mates since.

I didn't have to do it. But with Bill, because of the way he treats people, people like me, he commands our respect. That's how we are. We look after each other.

Bill the Manager

He was very funny, very passionate and actually not too shabby as a manager. His knowledge of football is extensive. He's very, very clued up. I think if he had wanted to, he could have probably progressed further if his life had taken a different path. When we finished the Woodhatch FC days, he carried on helping with the youngsters, bringing the younger kids through; it's his life. The effort he puts in is phenomenal.

Bill's not big for going out drinking and that social side of things. Football has always been the most important part of his life, whether that be West Ham, managing or coaching, whatever he's ever done, that's been the main part for him, and he always puts in 100 percent.

I'll always remember one thing that Bill used to say, not regularly, but it did stick in my mind. While we'd be getting ready for the game in the changing rooms, he used to say, "Apparently one in 10 men is gay. Which one of you is it?" Little things like that. Bill's a funny, funny bloke.

I got banned when I was playing for getting sent off. I got involved in an altercation with a ref. It was very heated, but probably not my best move. Let's just say it wasn't for giving him verbals! Some of the games used to be very competitive, put it that way.

We had a little bit of a reputation our team, not terrible, but we weren't scared of a physical game.

There was a meeting at the Town Hall with the FA, and my ban was coming up. I can't remember the reason why now, but it was a year's ban and they wanted to extend it for another year.

Bill and I were sitting in the Town Hall, near the stage, for my disciplinary hearing.

Bill spoke up for me saying that he'd be willing to give them a six-figure sum as a guarantee that I wouldn't get booked or get into trouble anymore, and that they shouldn't give me the additional year ban.

The bloke from the FA looked over the top of his glasses at Bill. "Mr Gardner," he said, "we do not run this league like the mafia!" I'd like to say there was a happy ending, but I got another year's ban. I wasn't allowed to play, but I still went to the matches and still supported the team. You still felt part of the team. Bill had a lot to do with that as well.

Reputations

At that time, it was when the football thing, especially in London, was all about who the top boys were and all that. Well for me, it was Bill Gardner and West Ham, they were the first. In later years I've met a lot of the other known faces from all the other teams, mainly through Cass.

But I've met most of them and Bill's held in such high regard it's unbelievable. I think most people - there's gonna be a few who can't stand him - but I think most people all agree Bill was the start of that movement. He never aspired to be that. I think it's just because of how loyal he was, how game he was, and how with his charisma, he's a leader, not a follower.

I think Bill was the first recognised person in terms of being known as a 'top boy'.

I've met loads. Barrington at Birmingham has a big presence, Boatsy at Forest, to name a few, I've met most of them. I've had drinks with Boatsy in Marbella which was pretty cool. It's like a little club now, where we've all been through the same terrace experiences and most of us can sit down and have a chat, and even a laugh about the old days.

There's certainly mutual respect between the old boys from the terraces.

In Bill's era, I think there was proper respect for people and, within each club, a respect for the elders, the top boys.

Things have changed, and not for the better. I haven't been to football now for years. You sort of move on. I think a lot of people have lost their interest in the game. The money in the game, the lack of respect from the players and the clubs towards the fans; you'll never get back what we had in the '70s and early '80s.

I think the ICF were the first properly organised firm. They were also pioneers. They were the first firm to start doing a lot of things. For me, at the time, they were the best dressed when the fashions side of it came in and became a part of it. West Ham were always at forefront of most things that happened at that time.

I kind of drifted into the terrace scene.

The experiences you go through weren't always great. You're going to end up in some near life-threatening situations - it felt like that at the time - which inevitably gave you a very strong bond between you and the people you stood with week after week.

It's a strong bond. I suppose it was only a matter of time before the original top boys started thinking, "Right, that's it, I'm done with this," and started becoming mates.

From Loftus Road to Upton Park

Because of my friendship with Bill and then Cass, I made quite a few trips to Upton Park. On one occasion with QPR we went over there and I said to our lads, "Look, you know I know Bill and Cass, well, they're gonna have a drink with us before the game."

We got out at Upton Park station. There were about 20 of us. We walked past the ground. It was known that we were coming over, and that nothing was to happen to us. We went to a bar, had a drink, Bill and Cass came in and we a good old time.

The Trial

I was with Bill all through that time. I remember going round to Bill's mum and dad's house. The conversations were like, "Bill, why are you like that? Why do you do the things you do?" His dad at the time was also quite ill.

I do remember his mum having a go at him about bringing someone round to the house because she didn't have her wig on.

It's a bit hazy now, but that was either while the case was going on or just before he got raided.

When he broke his leg he still went to West Ham, so I used to drive him. Now and again, I would go to watch West Ham with Bill. I probably took him to most games at that time.

I think maybe at the time it was a bit of a light-bulb moment, or a reality check for him. I visited him in prison and, put it this way, prison isn't for Bill. I used to take Sarah to Brixton and that's probably the most vulnerable I ever saw him. He looked defeated for the first time since I've known him. He was convinced they were going down. Even though there was a trial ahead I think he thought they'd decided already. Thatcher was making a point.

He was starting to put sort of plans into place that he wasn't going to be about for the next 10 years. I think in his head it was a done deal.

I remember - again this is going back a bit - I think he got taken to the hospital by the Old Bill and they still had him handcuffed when he was visiting his old man, just before he died. They still kept him handcuffed in front of his old man who was lying on his deathbed. I'll never forget that. You wouldn't wish that on anyone.

That's a lot of things to happen to anyone at the time. He said to me once, "I dunno why they're bothering with the trial, we've already been set-up as the scapegoats for everything, and we'll be the ones they are going to use."

The government wanted them, and they were going to be made an example of. That was the end of it.

He was trying to put things in place to make sure Sarah and his boys were looked after because he was going away for a long time. He asked me to make sure they were OK.

At the time it was more for moral support, but for a person that I held in such high esteem, who knew he could put his trust in me to look after the most loved people in his life was humbling.

It was not easy seeing him like that. I wouldn't have said this back then, but we're a little further down the road now. I would say he was one of the main ones who was least looking forward to getting bird, not that any of them were, but Bill was settled with Sarah and the boys. He had a lot to lose. It's one of them sort of things where you're doing something that's against the law. But it's against the written law, not the social law of our world.

It's the same as some of the England games - you'd go to away games, and the English papers slaughtered the England fans sometimes. But sometimes from the time you'd landed to the time you came home, you'd had to fight day and night because you'd been permanently under attack.

So, it was one of those sorts of things. You didn't have to do it, but you put yourself in that situation where you knew or thought you might have to.

35

A Trial, A Death & Abandonment

Undercover Metropolitan Police officers infiltrated the West Ham travelling fanbase for around 18 months as part of 'Operation Full Time' in the late 1980s. On January 20th 1987, the initiative culminated in a series of dawn raids across London and the home counties. Police identified Bill as the ICF's 'leader', while Ted and Cass were also arrested. Twelve months earlier, similar raids had landed some members of Chelsea's supporters with 10 year prison sentences. Bill was convinced the same fate awaited for him and his fellow defendants.

However, the trial of the West Ham 11, at Snaresbrook Magistrates Court in 1988, collapsed spectacularly, following the emergence of police fabrication of notebooks upon which the case against the defendants largely lay. The accusations were upheld after the defendants paid for forensic ESDA tests which concluded the police notebooks revealed large-scale inconsistencies in the dates and times entries were made. Many did not match the dates of events they purported to witness. The trial was thrown out as a result. Yet, despite having no case to answer and no further police action pending, Bill and his co-defendants received unilateral life-time bans from West Ham United.

The decline of trouble at games started the '80s - after the police raids. Chelsea got done first, and a few of them got 10 years. Then they came for us, and Margaret Thatcher wanted the law and order vote for the election. She wanted football fans to have ID cards too. It was all a vote-catcher because every week you'd read about more trouble. It was also an election year.

In truth, I never saw anyone who didn't want to get a clump, get a clump. If you were there, you knew why you were, and the people who wanted it got it. The really bad years were from 1967 to 1985. Once the swoops happened a lot of people had a rethink and thought hold on, this ain't for me. They just backed out. I'd already knocked it on the head when my boy James was born. I didn't want him to be without a dad. I didn't want to go and eat shit in prison and piss in a bucket. I didn't want him growing up with that stigma of *'your dad's in prison'*. When I was on remand at Brixton, Sarah brought him along and I wish she hadn't had done.

It upset me. I'm not one of these air-headed people that think I'm tough cos I'm in prison. I didn't want to be there full-stop. I didn't want to be with some of the half-wits I was with, though some of them were decent. I didn't want him growing up with that. Since then I've been on the straight and narrow.

I was eventually released on bail for £35k. A mate called Lee Jones put his house up to raise £25,000 for me, while Sarah's dad put up the other £10,000. People know I won't let them down. I won't abscond, I don't run away, I'll face the music; whatever the tune. I never saw Lee again, but I made sure I thanked him.

I was in there for about eight days. All the others were in the Scrubs, I think. I was the only one in Brixton. The old cliché of 'innocent till proven guilty', forget it. That went out the window. As soon as you get nicked, they look at you like you're guilty all the way through it. I was in plaster because I'd broken my leg and was struggling to shower and all that because of the plaster going soft. One of the screws in there brought in a plastic bag and some gaffer tape, so I managed to have a shower like that. He was a decent fella to be fair. There are good people about. There's a lot of lying bastards as well. When the Old Bill come round that morning - I think there was about 10 or 11 who nicked me – I said, "Alright lads, want a cup of tea?" When it got to court half of them denied it. How was he upon arrest? "Oh, he was really aggressive!" Then one of them went in the dock and said, "Yeah, he was alright, he offered us a cuppa." You could see the jury thinking hang on, this don't sound right.

When I was going from the prison to my second hearing, where I got bail, I had my personal stuff with me; including a bar of chocolate. I gave that bar of chocolate to the coppers escorting me in the van. I don't know why I did that, but he looked at me like I was a fucking bear with two heads! To be fair, I've always found police officers a little strange, but I've always treated them with respect. And the West Ham coppers know this with me. I will always be civil. I don't like them, don't get me wrong. But I will never let them say I haven't got any class. Even the bloke who tried to stitch me up, the copper who was leading the case. He later got a job at West Ham as head of security. I always treated him civilly. I always spoke to him when my ban was lifted, and I always asked how his wife was because she weren't very well. I think that puzzled him. They used to go away thinking, "Why's he like this? Why's he not telling me to fuck off." It's just the way I am.

A lot of water goes under the bridge and you have to forget it and play the cards you're dealt. I've been pulled up about it loads of times by my great mate, Ted. "Why do you talk to them?" he says to me. And I say, "Why not?" I won't let them have the last laugh by saying what a horrible, fucking violent bastard that man is. I won't let them do it.

I never spoke to my mum and dad about what I was getting up to at football, but I think they had a fair idea. They never brought it up. They knew I didn't mind a fight. My dad was disappointed in me though when it came to court. He was totally convinced I was guilty. He wouldn't believe that a policeman would make up lies, or in our case six to eight police officers. Like I said, I did it years before, but that wasn't what they got me for.

But yeah, my dad was disappointed, really disappointed.

I'm not sure about my mum, to be fair. I don't think she cared one way or the other.

It got worse when I had to go to the hospital to see him during the trial. He was in a bad way. On one occasion they made me go to the hospital with two uniformed court officials with me. My dad didn't like that, and it was completely unnecessary. They weren't Old Bill, they were just court officers. I was on bail and not breached any conditions, so they could have let me go and see my dad on my own.

When I got bailed out, I got £35,330 compensation, which was ridiculous because you had murderers getting let out on £20,000 bail back then.

Trial

The trial lasted 16 weeks and two days at Snaresbrook. But before that, two weeks was spent giving evidence at Stratford Magistrates Court at the committal proceedings. So they had to tell the court everything they had on you. There were loads of people: police, witnesses against me, the prosecutor. I thought, "I've got no chance here, I've had it." It was just another battle I had to try and win but I'll be honest and say, for the first time in my life, ever since I was that scared, bullied, abused kid, I didn't fancy my chances one bit.

When I turned up for the Snaresbrook trial and met my fellow defendants, I didn't know half of them. They knew me or of me, but I didn't know them. I sat in the third seat and they started presenting their evidence, which was genuinely a pile of shit. I decided from day one I wasn't just going to sit there hour after hour listening to what was being said, so I wrote loads of notes. I wrote everyone's name and I used to put a cross against bad points and a tick against good points that were made during the trial.

I'd think, "That's wrong, that didn't happen," so I kept a record of what was going on. After they'd given their evidence - which was a borderline joke - I started to think we might be in a half-decent position. When it came to us giving evidence, Cass went in first, followed by me.

I'd already seen the way the prosecutor, Vivian Robinson, had treated Cass, so I was ready for him.

The way they all talked to Cass was designed to make him lose his rag. Cass' brief was very old. He represented the Krays, that's how old he was. Robinson really laid into Cass, partly I believe because of the colour of Cass' skin.

They spoke to him like he was a piece of shit. They may as well have said, "Here's the guilty Mr Cass Pennant, who's also a piece of shit." It wound me up no end. It made me angry they spoke to him like that. Here we were, fighting for our lives, and some jumped up old fart thinks he can talk to my mate like that.

When it was my time to go in I took a slightly different approach. When they asked me questions, I made sure they got a full answer. I didn't give them any 'yes' and 'no' answers. They're very clever people and none of us could match them for intelligence. We knew that, so we had to box clever.

I gave them the longest answers I possibly could, so I had time to think about what the next question was going to be.

They'd try and butt in when I was giving an answer so I'd say, "Mr. Robinson, you've asked me a question, will you please allow me to answer," or in other words, "shut the fuck up and let me speak."

I used to watch them speaking to each other. I'd look at the jury, trying to sus out their body language. One or two of them looked sympathetic towards us, while the youngsters in the jury didn't even want to be there and were clearly bored out of their brains. It wasn't that exciting a trial to be fair.

But the people who I felt were most on our side were the older jurors. We found that out at the end. One of the older ladies on the jury told me at the end of the case, "We found you all innocent before you gave your evidence because you could see their case was based on a pack of lies." She told me that at the end of the trial, outside the court after the case collapsed.

One dinnertime during the trial, some of the boys went into the pub across the road while the jurors were in there having lunch. The boys weren't to know, but the jurors reported it to the judge. I never used to go to the pub. I used to go out through the back door, sit in the car and have a sandwich. After that sequence of events, that led to them being in the pub with the jurors, they stopped us going out at dinner times, so we were down in the cells every lunchtime.

The boys were as silly as arseholes, going over and chatting to the birds on the jury. That was never gonna happen. I called them cunts for doing that in the position we were all in. I did think it was gonna damage our chances. It weren't the brightest way to be carrying on when you're looking at a 10-year stretch. By the time I was done with them, they knew not to set foot in there again. And they didn't.

People make mistakes, it's part of life and you can't dwell on it.

But I could've murdered them, which would've been a strange twist at my own trial. I never went in that pub once, and I never went in when the trial ended either. When the trial ended, I got in my car and I came straight home.

Like I said, we weren't on the same intellectual level as the prosecutor, the QC's, the lawyers, otherwise we'd be down there and they'd be in the dock.

Early Predictions

At the beginning I thought we had no hope. I honestly thought we were fucked and there was no getting out of a 10-year stretch. I just thought we'll go through this and we'll get 10 years. That's what we were looking at. The Chelsea lot had been banged up a year earlier. It was on the strength of what we did in our trial that they got out soon after our's had been thrown out, and they got their compensation money.

I've got to know a couple of them Chelsea lads since then, good luck to them. It was all political. The whole trial, everything was political. Margaret Thatcher was using us as part of her 'vote for me, I'll stamp out crime in this country' strategy. It was an election year as well, but in all fairness, at football it wasn't good, it wasn't getting any better. There was more and more trouble going on all the time and I could see where they were coming from, to an extent.

But instead of doing the job properly, and getting the ones who were still active, they just went for names. They went for names, not crimes. They went for names at all the clubs; Chelsea included. People who were well-known names over there got their collar felt. They did the same with us. I'd like to know, when they carried out those raids on all the clubs, whether it was a matter of names and faces, rather than crimes committed. We were targets. They used us as targets. And to be fair to ya, on the events they were supposed to have had after 18 months surveillance; I could've got a better case up against them in 6 weeks. It was that pathetic.

They lied, made things up, and invented situations which never arose. At one point the jury was told, "When Bill waves the axe, that's the signal to attack. When the axe starts shining in the sunlight." That was supposed to have happened after one particular away game.

My QC asked, "What was he wearing?" Apparently, I had a t-shirt and tracksuit bottoms on. So where am I keeping this fucking axe?

It was like a comedy film. When they said it everyone just laughed. They'd never heard such a stupid story. Can you honestly visualise me standing on a hill with the sun shining and a fucking great big axe above my head at ten to five on a Saturday afternoon. Paint me face blue and I could've been Braveheart!

Abandonment

West Ham banned all of us for four years between 86-90. They didn't wait for the trial. They banned us the minute we were nicked. During the trial, the West Ham commercial manager, Brian Blower, commented he had attended a meeting with 'our leader'. Everyone asked who this 'leader' was.

He had allegedly replied, "Margaret Thatcher," the implication being there'd been communication between Number 10 and the Club. Football hooliganism had officially arrived as a political issue, after the sociologists and criminologists had got it so wrong.

I think it might have been one of the other boys – Paul Dorset's brief – who wanted to establish the time, date, minutes and outcome of the meeting Brian Blower had referred to. Maggie didn't want to deal with it, but she had no choice. The terrace movement was now very much in the public's consciousness. And Cass had been on Wogan for fuck's sake!

Bereavement

He was dying; my dad was dying in the hospice he was in. He was in a terrible state during the trial. We didn't really talk about it. I'd just sit there and hold his hand. He couldn't really have a conversation, but he knew I was there. And in his mind I was as guilty as the day is long, simple as that.

I never would be able to tell him that, not only was I not guilty, but it took a load of lying coppers to nick us in the first place and put us all through hell. In hindsight, I'm glad I didn't have the chance to tell him. A world where coppers tell porkies to frame innocent people ain't one he would have recognised, or liked.

In terms of the trial's impact, the biggest thing for me was the ban, because I didn't think I deserved the ban. And it was all I ever did; football was all I ever did. So to not be able to do it, was a huge part of my life gone.

I don't want to be made out to be Mother Theresa. I did it. But I did it years before they arrested me. When they arrested me, I'd been packed up for a long while. Once my James was born, I had no involvement with any of it. I kept away, I kept myself to myself.

I didn't want James growing up without a dad.

36

Regret

It was when I was back home that I met my first wife, Leslie, watching the football at Upton Park – where else! I ended up marrying her two years later, when I was 18, after she became pregnant with my first child and only daughter, Kelly. I made the mistake of telling my mum before I went round to talk to Leslie's parents. I was going to tell them I'd do right by her daughter and marry her. That's how it was back then. But my mum 'very kindly' contacted Leslie's parents before I could.

"Do you know your daughter is pregnant by my son?" my mum screamed at them down the phone. So, I had the welcoming committee at the door when I got there. I was doing the decent thing. I was going to marry her. We'd moved in together. Maybe that was a mistake, because I wasn't meant to be with Leslie and we split up two years later.

That caused a skirmish with her family, who didn't want me to divorce her. They were very strict, and her grandmother put up £800 to have my knees done in. I don't think they wanted it coming out that she'd cheated on me. A gentleman turned up at my mum's house looking for me a few weeks later. My mum told him I was down the pub. He tracked me down and walked up to me in the boozer.

"You Bill Gardner?" he asked.

"Yeah," I said, "who are you?"

"I want to have a word with you," he said.

I walked outside with him. As soon as we did the street was filled with lights. My mum had called the police because she thought it was dodgy. For the second time that night, I got asked if I was Bill Gardner.

"Yeah, that's me," I told the copper. He looked me up and down.

"Are you alright?"

I looked at the bloke stood next to me, the one who'd been round my mum's house.

"Yeah, yeah, I'm alright, I'm just talking to my mate here."

"Your mum phoned us worried about you."

"Oh, don't worry, she's always doing that," I told the copper.

The bloke looking to do my knees in looked at me, winked, got in his car and I never saw him again.

Holding my Hands Up

Not long after splitting up with Leslie, I was introduced to Janice, who came from East Ham. We hit it off straight away, and she became my second wife. We were together for 10 years and she was a lovely girl. That's what makes saying sorry so hard.

When I was with Janice I cheated on her with Sarah - the mother of my two beloved boys - and the woman who's put up with me for the last 37 years. If it weren't for Sarah, I'd be in prison or dead. I know that's a cliché. I fucking hate clichés. But it's true, so what can I say. But I regret doing that to Janice because I loved her. I just felt our lack of having kids was driving us apart. She was a good person, so yeah, there's regret there. I didn't handle it too well. I gave her nearly everything I had when she left. I left myself with nothing. I don't know if she'll read this, or if she'll even want to read it, but I regret the way it ended. Although it was for the best; maybe for both of us.

Whatever the circumstances, the fact is I was cheating on Janice, there's no way around that. Sarah was in hospital having my oldest boy and I went in there to finish with her because I felt it wasn't right. I'd cheated on Janice. When I saw Sarah lying in the hospital bed with my new son, I couldn't do it.

I'm a loyal person, so in a way, I mugged myself off with the way I treated Janice. I hate hurting people, and I hate seeing people hurt. So, I know what I did was wrong. I just hope, if she is reading this, she knows how sorry I am for cheating on her. I'm a loyal person. I don't cheat on people - I did then - but not seeing my daughter, not contacting her enough, and cheating on Janice are things I'll never forgive myself for. I wasn't a nice person back then compared to the man I am now. My life took me to a place now where I'm as happy as I can be, given my past.

Sarah's a great girl. She's been fantastic for me. But so was Janice, who I truly loved. I hope she's doing well.

Kelly

Time is a big thing and my time is going quick. I don't want to die with Kelly thinking her dad abandoned her, that he fucked off with somebody else, because it wasn't quite like that. Loyalty's a two-way street, and in that relationship with Leslie it was only coming one way, from me. I just want to leave it at that.

I love her like a dad should love his daughter. I done it all wrong, and if I could go back, I would do it completely different. But I didn't do it right. I was 18 years old. I wasn't very bright, and at the time I felt it was better to have her mum and not her dad. Certain things happened that made me think I didn't want to go and see her because there would be more rows, and more upset. I didn't want that. I didn't want that for anyone.

In fairness, the only loser was Kelly. My door is always open to her. I'm still her dad and, if she feels I did the wrong thing I'll take that. But it wasn't the way I wanted it to end, and I suspect she's probably been told a few things about me that aren't too complimentary. However, my biggest regret was not keeping in contact with her. I wanted the little girl to forget me because she was only a baby at the time and because I could see only heartbreak for her, which is something I have lived with myself. But my door's always open to her. She's my flesh and blood, and always will be.

Printed in Great Britain
by Amazon